AMERICAN HISTORY

The Constitution and Founding of America

John M. Dunn

LUCENT BOOKS

An imprint of Thomson Gale, a part of The Thomson Corporation

THOMSON

GALE

Detroit • New York • San Francisco • New Haven, Conn. • Waterville, Maine • London

© 2007 Thomson Gale, a part of The Thomson Corporation.
Thomson and Star Logo are trademarks and Gale and Lucent Books are registered trademarks used herein under license.
For more information, contact
Lucent Books
27500 Drake Rd.
Farmington Hills, MI 48331-3535
Or you can visit our Internet site at http://www.gale.com

LIBRARY OF CONGRESS CATALOGING-IN-PUBLICATION DATA

Dunn, John M., 1949–
  The Constitution and founding of America / by John M. Dunn.
    p. cm. (American history)
  Includes bibliographical references and index.
  ISBN 978-1-59018-956-6 (hardcover)
  1. United States. Constitution—Juvenile literature. 2. United
States—Politics and government—1775–1783—Juvenile literature. 3. United
States—Politics and government—1783–1789—Juvenile literature. 4.
Constitutional history—United States—Juvenile literature. 5. United
States—History—Colonial period, ca. 1600-1775—Juvenile literature. I.
Title.
  E303.D86 2007
  320.973—dc22
                                                              2007015976

ISBN-10: 1-59018-956-6

Printed in the United States of America

Contents

Foreword

The United States has existed as a nation for just over 200 years. By comparison, Rome existed as a nation-state for more than 1000 years. Out of a few struggling British colonies, the United States developed relatively quickly into a world power whose policy decisions and culture have great influence on the world stage. What events and aspirations drove this young American nation to such great heights in such a short period of time? The answer lies in a close study of its varied and unique history. As James Baldwin once remarked, "American history is longer, larger, more various, more beautiful, and more terrible than anything anyone has ever said about it."

The basic facts of United States history— names, dates, places, battles, treaties, speeches, and acts of Congress—fill countless textbooks. These facts, though essential to a thorough understanding of world events, are rarely compelling for students. More compelling are the stories in history, the experience of history.

Titles in this series explore the history of the country and the experiences of Americans. What influences led the colonists to risk everything and break from Britain? Who was the driving force behind the Constitution? Which factors led thousands of people to leave their homelands and settle in the United States? Questions like these do not have simple answers; by discussing them, however, we can view the past as a more real, interesting, and accessible place.

Students will find excellent tools for research and investigation in every title. Lucent Books' American History series provides not only facts, but also the analysis and context necessary for insightful critical thinking about history and about current events. Fully cited quotations from historical figures, eyewitnesses, letters, speeches, and writings bring vibrancy and authority to the text. Annotated bibliographies allow students to evaluate and locate sources for further investigation. Sidebars highlight important and interesting figures, events, or related primary source excerpts. Timelines, maps, and full color images add another dimension of accessibility to the stories being told.

It has been said the past has a history of repeating itself, for good and ill. In these pages, students will learn a bit about both and, perhaps, better understand their own place in this world.

Important Dates at the Time of the

1498
Spain settles some two hundred colonists on the Caribbean island now known as the Dominican Republic.

1543
Nicolaus Copernicus asserts that Earth revolves around the sun.

1602
Batholomew Gosnold explores "New England," the area from Maine to Cape Cod. He is the first Englishman to explore the region.

1607
First British settlement at Jamestown is established.

1400	1500	1600

1609
Shakespeare's sonnets first published.

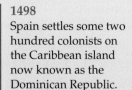

1675
The pocket watch is developed.

1690
English philosopher John Locke publishes his "Essay Concerning Human Understanding."

1630
Puritans establish the Massachusetts Bay Colony.

1649
British king Charles I found guilty of treason by the British Parliament and executed.

AN
ESSAY
CONCERNING
Humane Understanding.

In Four BOOKS.

Quam bellum est velle confiteri potius nescire quod nescias, quam ista effutientem nauseare, atque ipsum sibi displicere! Cic. de Natur. Deor. l. 1.

LONDON:
Printed by *Eliz. Holt,* for **Thomas Basset,** at the *George in Fleetstreet,* near St. *Dunstan's Church.* MDCXC.

Constitution and Founding of America

1720
China takes control of Tibet.

1742
Russian pogroms kill thousands of Jews.

1739
Great Awakening gets underway.

1776
U.S. Congress approves the Declaration of Independence.

1700   **1800**   **1900**

1804
Meriwether Lewis and William Clark set out on their exploration of the Louisiana Territory.

1789
United States ratifies the Bill of Rights; the French Assembly adopts the Declaration of the Rights of Man.

1783
United States and Great Britain sign peace treaty in September.

The Great Experiment

The United States is the one of the most powerful countries in history—one whose military might dwarfs all others. Representing only 5 percent of the world's population, Americans have also created one of the world's wealthiest countries, thanks to the nation's long traditions of free markets, hard work, entrepreneurialism, and democratically elected government. The American economy is, in fact, a powerful international economic engine. In addition, the United States boasts the most influential representative democracy on earth, serving as a model for many other nations.

These successes were made possible because the United States is also something else—an ongoing experiment in self-government, launched in 1776 on the proposition that people can and must govern themselves. At the core of this experiment is the U.S. Constitution, a document that safeguards individual liberties, provides a blueprint for governance, and puts limits on power.

The nation's roots extend to thirteen British colonies in North America, which by the mid-eighteenth century were populated by fewer than 4 million people. By this time, a growing rift—one born of social, political, economic, cultural, and geographic differences—threatened to split the colonies from England. The deepening divide was made worse by British mismanagement and miscalculation. American behavior also contributed to the strife. In violation of royal policy, American settlers kept intruding into Native American lands west of the Allegheny Mountains. American colonists also angered the British by objecting to paying for their own military protection on the grounds that "taxation without representation was tyranny."

Meanwhile, increasing numbers of Americans were convinced that British authorities were depriving them of their rights as British citizens—rights gained by the British people through centuries of toil and bloodshed that made them the freest people in the world.

Fueling the fires of American discontent were the radical ideas of an intellectual movement ignited in England and France called the Enlightenment. Writers

The U.S. Constitution protects individual liberties, helps provide guidance, and puts restraints on power.

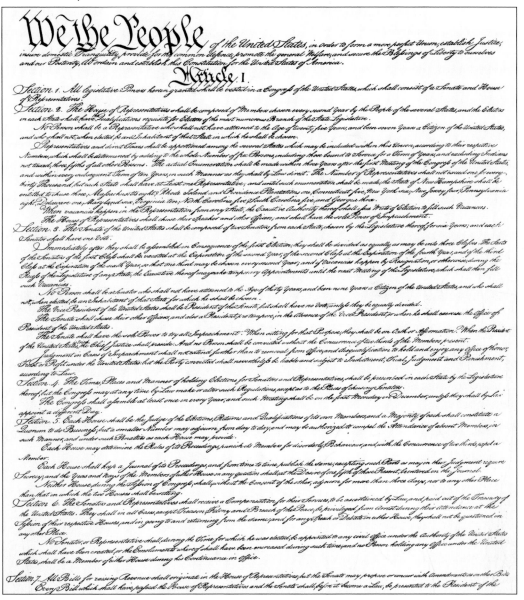

of this movement celebrated the power of human reason, not superstition or blind obedience to tradition and authority, as the best way to solve society's problems. Such ideas fell upon fertile soil in colonial America.

Irreconcilable differences between England and its colonies finally resulted in the American Revolution, a bloody war that lasted six years. Under the military leadership of George Washington, American troops ultimately defeated the most powerful empire in the world in 1781.

The Revolution, however, did not end with England's departure from American soil. The new nation now had to forge a new government. Fifty-five of America's most accomplished leaders met in Philadelphia in 1787, and conceived a bold plan for a new government called the U.S. Constitution. This plan drew on both the wisdom of the past and the intellectual excitement of the Enlightenment to create the foundation for a government that divided power among its institutions and protected personal liberties.

Despite their best efforts, most if not all the framers of the Constitution believed the final draft was flawed. So did millions of other Americans in the com-

ing years. By design the original Constitution ignored the rights of blacks, women, Native Americans, indentured servants, and white males who had no property. It did not outlaw slavery—an institution that led to civil war in 1861.

The framers of the Constitution, however, foresaw the need for future generations to adapt the Constitution to changing times. To facilitate this, they provided constitutional means of making amendments to the document itself. Judges, too, have had to keep the Constitution current by interpreting contemporary issues based on the spirit and intent of the framers. As a result of these actions, America's most important document survives today as a "living constitution," able to grow and evolve over time.

The Constitution serves another purpose. Once the mortar that bound thirteen sovereign colonies into a new nation, it today unites 300 million people in fifty states and provides them with a common national identity.

Challenges and fights over the meaning and purpose of the Constitution are ever present. History indicates, however, that the Constitution empowers Americans to remedy these problems and "form a more perfect Union."

Chapter One

The Emergence of the Thirteen Colonies

The story of the United States begins with the arrival of Christopher Columbus in the Americas in 1492. It was a discovery that sparked a three-hundred-year-long land rush. To Europe's ruling classes, the New World, as the Americas were known, offered riches and opportunities they could not ignore.

European Competition in America

Nations, however, were not prepared to share the New World. Only two years after Columbus's discovery, Pope Alexander IV, head of the Roman Catholic Church, decreed that the Americas should be divided between two Catholic nations, Spain and Portugal.

Other European powers, however, paid little heed to the pope's proclamation. "Show me the clause in [the biblical] Adam's will by which he divided the world between my brothers of Spain and Portugal," exclaimed the French king Francis I.[1]

Soon Sweden, the Netherlands, France, England, and the Danish Kingdom (which then included Norway and Iceland) dispatched small sailing ships for America. Explorers, soldiers, treasure seekers, adventurers, and priests were among the first to arrive. Next came immigrants that farmed, fished, hunted, trapped, and set up communities and commercial enterprises. They carried with them firearms, horses, iron cooking pots, writing utensils, and other artifacts of interest to Native Americans.

Some Europeans befriended and peacefully coexisted with America's inhabitants, the Indians, as Columbus mistakenly called them. All too often, however, encounters between Europeans and Native Americans resulted in violence. Making matters worse, new diseases introduced by the Europeans killed millions of Native Americans. Equipped with superior weapons and armies, an ever-growing immigrant population increasingly pushed

In 1492 Christopher Columbus arrived in the Americas, beginning the story of the United States.

Native Americans off their tribal lands and seized them.

By the seventeenth century, several European nations were well anchored in North America. Spain controlled Texas, California, the far West, Central America, and much of South America. Scandinavians settled parts of the Northeast. French fur trappers, merchants, and Catholic priests occupied the Great Plains in settlements ranging from Québec in the north to New Orleans on the Gulf Coast.

England's Colonies

England, meanwhile, set up thriving colonies along the Atlantic coast. Its first permanent colony was Jamestown, Virginia, established in 1607. At first, Jamestown's investors expected to earn a profit by finding valuable metals and other riches. Soon, however, the colony was headed for disaster. Almost half the settlers died from disease and starvation during the first year. If not for the strong leadership of Captain John Smith the colony would have collapsed. To succeed, the settlers had to abandon seeking gold and instead build a stable community with a new sense of direction and purpose. To do this, they enticed skilled tradesmen from England with offers of free land. Colonists tried other ways to earn a profit, such as marketing cedar and sassafras. Eventually, they found a profitable commodity—tobacco.

Those who left England did so because they believed they would live more prosperous lives in Virginia. However, they

A Jamestown settler shares his small supply of corn. Initially spending most of their time searching for gold, the first Jamestown colonists soon began to run out of food. To survive, they had to focus on building a strong community instead of looking for gold.

did not wish to forgo their rights as citizens of England. To assure that their status would not change in the New World, the colony's new charter provided the assurance that all British people and their children born there "Shall have and enjoy all liberties, franchises, and immunities . . . as if they had been abiding and born, within our realm of England."[2]

A very different British settlement began far to the north of Virginia in 1620.

These America-bound travelers had originally sailed for Virginia, but stormy weather forced them north to Plymouth, Massachusetts. Although the land there was colder and less hospitable than Virginia, the voyagers decided to stay where they had landed. Among the 102 on board were 35 religious dissenters, who called themselves Pilgrims. They were members of the Puritan movement that strove to "purify" the Church of England

Colonists originally set sail for Virginia, but arrived in Plymouth, Massachusetts, instead as a result of bad weather.

of any Catholic tradition, such as robes worn by priests or images of the Virgin Mary and Catholic saints.

Before coming ashore, however, forty-one people agreed to sign and abide by a covenant with God that required each of them to work and provide for the common good. This Mayflower Compact, as the agreement became known, was the first document of self-government in the New World.

The community at Plymouth was later absorbed into the Massachusetts Bay Colony, founded in 1630 by a much larger group of Puritans who escaped persecution in England. Their leader, lawyer John Winthrop, had proclaimed, "We shall be as a city upon a hill. The eyes of all people are upon us."[3]

Forty-one individuals signed the Mayflower Compact, the first document of self-government in the New World.

British Colonization Spreads

Other British colonies were established, most of them with strong religious ties. Dissenters from the Massachusetts Bay Colony founded Connecticut in 1636 and began moving into Rhode Island a year later. Others broke away and settled in New Hampshire in 1638. Despite their religious differences, these New England colonies shared many common Protestant beliefs. Religious freedom for Catholics, meanwhile, was the driving force behind a colony founded by Lord Baltimore in Maryland in 1634.

In 1664 England took control of the Dutch colony of New Netherlands, which they renamed New York, and New Jersey, an area that contained both Dutch and Swedish settlements. Seventeen years later, Pennsylvania began as a religious haven for Quakers. Delaware, another area with Swedish and Dutch settlers, was ruled by the Pennsylvania legislature until 1701 when its citizens created their own representative assembly.

To the south of Virginia lay Carolina, once a French Protestant settlement named after King Charles IX of France. It, too, fell to the British and later split into North and South Carolina. Below South Carolina lay Georgia, a colony begun in 1732 by philanthropist James Oglethorpe who created a haven for those who would otherwise be imprisoned in England for unpaid debts. Georgia was also a military outpost established to keep watch on its southern neighbor Florida, a Spanish possession.

Altogether, England boasted thirteen colonies, and immigrants poured into them. In fact, between 1660 and 1770, three-quarters of a million Europeans resettled in North America. They were not all from the British Isles (England, Wales, Scotland, and Ireland). Immigrants also came from France, Germany, Switzerland, the Netherlands, Sweden, and Finland.

Throngs of desperate people were eager to leave the Old World. Many were sick of cruel, arbitrary laws imposed by royal tyrants. Peasant men dreaded being drafted into political wars and sold as mercenaries to various monarchs. Europeans everywhere despised religious persecution and the religious wars of 1618–1648. Widespread poverty in England was made worse when legions of farm workers lost their jobs as landowners converted their vast holdings to sheep grazing instead of growing crops.

Not all immigrants came to America as free people. Some freely sold themselves as indentured servants who were obliged to work for merchants or artisans in the colonies for seven years and longer. Others were kidnapped and brought to North America against their will. Millions of blacks were captured in Africa and sold as slaves in America.

Most immigrants lived in towns and villages. However, cities were growing, too. Boston, Newport, New York, Charleston, Salem, Providence, Baltimore, Richmond, and Savannah were becoming important centers of trade and commerce. By 1774 Philadelphia, with forty thousand inhabitants, was the nation's largest and wealthiest city and the second biggest in the British Empire. An important port city with paved streets, sidewalks, whale-oil lamps, and police, Philadelphia was also the country's leading intellectual center.

Three Distinct Cultures

By the middle of the eighteenth century, the thirteen colonies had developed into three distinct regions. The northern, or New England, colonies resembled the British countryside. Inhabitants lived in towns and toiled on small subsistence farms. Others worked as lumbermen in vast forests or as shipbuilders, whalers, fishermen, and traders in bustling seacoast towns such as Portsmouth, Boston, and Providence.

In the Middle Colonies, meanwhile, fertile lands and a moderate climate allowed family farms to produce such vast amounts of grain that they became known as the Bread Colonies. Lengthy and navigable rivers, such as the Hudson and Delaware, along with natural harbors in New York and Philadelphia,

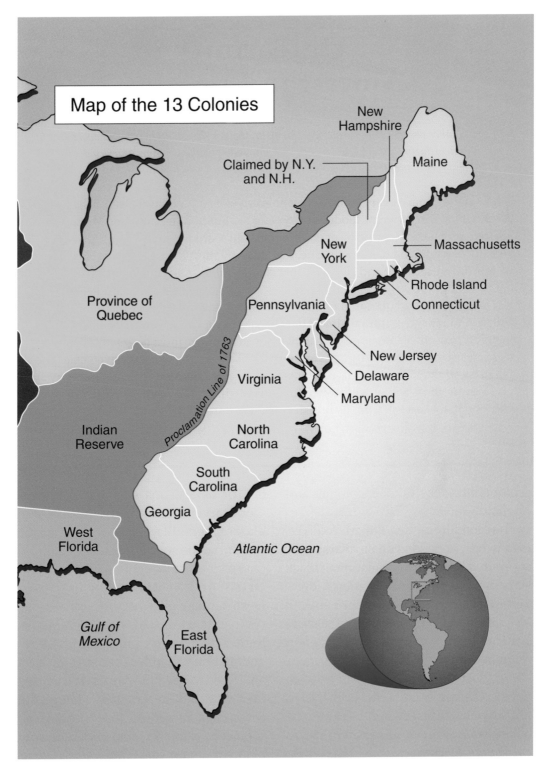

Map of the 13 Colonies

New Hampshire

Maine

Claimed by N.Y. and N.H.

Massachusetts

New York

Rhode Island
Connecticut

Province of Quebec

Pennsylvania

New Jersey

Delaware

Virginia

Maryland

Proclamation Line of 1763

Indian Reserve

North Carolina

South Carolina

Georgia

West Florida

Atlantic Ocean

Gulf of Mexico

East Florida

The Uniformity of American Speech

Like many other aspects of the American identity, the American language also evolved into something new during the colonial period. William Eddis, in a letter from America dated June 8, 1770, observes a distinctive sameness of speech developing and unifying Americans.

In England, almost every county is distinguished by a peculiar dialect; even different habits, and different modes of thinking . . . but in Maryland, and throughout adjacent provinces, it is worthy of observation, that a striking similarity of speech universally prevails; and it is strictly true, that the pronunciation of the generality of the people has an accuracy and elegance, that cannot fail of gratifying the most judicious ear.

The colonists are composed of adventurers, not only from every district of Great Britain and Ireland, but from almost every other European government. . . . Is it not, therefore, reasonable to suppose, that the English language must be greatly corrupted by such a strange intermixture of various nations? The reverse is, however, true. The language of the immediate descendants of such a promiscuous [mixed] ancestry is perfectly uniform, and unadulterated [uncorrupted]; nor has it borrowed any provincial, or national accent, from its British or foreign parentage.

Quoted in Daniel J. Boorstin, *The Americans: The Colonial Experience.* New York: Random House, 1958, pp. 274–75.

promoted trade with other colonies and England.

The economy of the southern colonies, meanwhile, depended on big plantations supported by a large population of black slaves who tended crops of rice, indigo, and tobacco. Much of southern society also mirrored the rigid British social class system. At the top were rich plantation owners whose families lived in mansions. Most southerners, however, were poor white farmers from the British Isles, who dwelled in shacks and cabins on the backwoods frontier. Others worked as carpenters, blacksmiths, bricklayers, bakers, or as artisans such as architects, woodcarvers, silversmiths, potters, and glassmakers. Black slaves lived at the bottom of the social order.

Similar Experiences

Despite their growing differences, the colonies had much in common. Colonial homes were commonly huddled together. Sanitation was often poor. Pigs and cattle roamed the streets. The wilderness was seldom far away. That meant town dwellers could leave home and soon enter a forest to fish or hunt to supplement their meals. Those who cleared homesteads far away from the established settlements worried constantly about Native American attacks and carried their muskets and rifles with them at all times. In many areas colonists formed armed militias to provide protection. These experiences prepared many colonists for military action when the American Revolution arrived.

Colonies also shared in their government. The king, or someone he selected, picked a governor to run each colony. In turn, the governor chose an upper council of lawmakers to make some of the laws. A select group of male colonists, however, was also allowed to elect a lower council of lawmakers. At first, most voters and office holders were either aristocrats or rich landowners. This practice was in accordance with a widely shared conviction that the wealth generated by land ownership enabled an individual to be truly free and not dependent on others for work and money. Such individuals, according to prevailing attitudes, were most fit to govern others.

Englishmen All

Although colonists lived far from England, most considered themselves British citizens who were entitled to the same rights as citizens in the British Isles.

King John (seated) signs the Magna Carta, also known as the Great Charter, in 1215.

No Rights for Blacks, Indians, and Mulattos

Though most colonists believed they were entitled to the rights of English citizens, few wanted to extend rights to slaves, Indians, or mulattos, as is made clear in this passage from a 1705 Virginia state statute:

And if any slave resist his master, or owner, or other person, by his or her order, correcting such slave, and shall happen to be killed in such correction, it shall not be accounted felony [a serious crime]; but the master, owner, and every such other person so giving correction, shall be free and acquit of all punishment and accusation for the same, as if such accident had never happened: And also, if any negro, mulatto, or Indian, bond or free, shall at any time, lift his or her hand, in opposition against any Christian, not being negro, mulatto, or Indian, he or she so offending, shall, for every such offence, proved by the oath of the party, receive on his her bare back, thirty lashes, well laid on, cognizable by a justice of the peace for that county wherein such offence shall be committed.

Quoted in John M. Blum, William S. McFeely, Edmund S. Morgan, Arthur M. Schlesinger Jr., Kenneth M. Stampp, and C. Vann Woodward, *The National Experience: A History of the United States*, 6th ed. San Diego: Harcourt Brace Jovanovich, 1985, p. 63.

These rights dated as far back as 1215 when King John signed the Great Charter, or Magna Carta, a document that required monarchs to obey the rule of law. It also established that all accused persons were entitled to a trial by jury and that only Parliament, an elected body, could levy taxes. In time, British courts and lawmakers guaranteed other rights. By the seventeenth century, for instance, no citizen could be unreasonably deprived of life, liberty, or property. The Habeas Corpus Act of 1679 stated that arrested persons had a right to receive an official statement of the charges against them and a right to a speedy trial. Another legal provision stipulated that authorities could not search a person's home without a search warrant obtained from a court. The 1689 British Bill of Rights asserted that monarchs could exercise certain powers only with the permission of the Parliament. Citizens were also entitled to ask their government to solve problems, and they enjoyed protection against excessive fines, bails, and cruel and unusual punishments.

Adapting British Law in the New World

Like other citizens within the British Empire, the colonists also wanted their lives regulated and protected by British common law—a code of legal decisions made by local county courts in England over the centuries. However, because trained lawyers were scarce in the New World, settlers simplified many of these old legal procedures. Americans also abolished the death penalty for petty theft, a punishment that was still carried out in England.

The Emergence of an American Identity

Though most Americans considered themselves British citizens, their lives developed quite differently than those of people in England. Unlike their British counterparts, Americans lived among growing numbers of immigrants, many of whom spoke other languages. Non-British immigrants made up as much as 40 percent of the colonial population. Their numbers included Germans, French, Dutch, Scots, Scotch-Irish, and Celtic Irish.

American colonial life was also filled with optimism, energy, and drive. Much of this dynamic way of living emerged from immigrants who, because they were restless and discontent with their old lives in Europe, came to America looking for adventure, opportunity, prosperity, and a new start. Here, too, they learned to be resourceful in an unknown continent populated with wild creatures and human beings far different from those they had known in the Old World. In time, the colonists developed their own accents, customs, values, and beliefs.

By the mid-eighteenth century, in fact, a distinctive American character had emerged in the colonies. Notes historian Richard B. Morris, "The colonial subjects of George III in 1775 were entirely different from those who had planted Virginia and Plymouth 150 years earlier in James I's reign."[4]

Religious Experience in a New Land

Religion helped forge this new American identity. It provided many Americans with a moral code, a sense of belonging, and a basis for a spiritual existence; however, darker impulses were also at work. Though colonists enjoyed

Preacher George Whitefield's emotional sermons helped bring about the Great Awakening.

more religious tolerance than anywhere in western Europe, discrimination and persecution were common. For instance, Catholics, Unitarians, and Jews were banned from voting or holding office in several colonies. In addition, many colonists saw no need to separate religion and government. Thus, the Anglican Church, or Church of England, became the official religion of New York, Virginia, Maryland, and North and South Carolina. The Congregational Church, meanwhile, was the official church of Massachusetts, New Hampshire, and Connecticut. However, no single religion ever reigned as the official religion of all the colonies. In fact, many American congregations exercised local control over their churches rather than yield to powerful religious authorities, as was the case in England. Some scholars believe such resistance to authority fostered democratic values that later contributed to the American independence movement.

Though many colonists, such as Anglicans and Puritans, were religiously conservative, other Americans, especially those living in rural areas, welcomed the more robust, emotional form of worship encouraged by evangelist preachers. One of the best known was British-born George Whitefield, who in 1739 traveled across Virginia, holding wild religious jubilees during which he declared that

The Wonders of Philadelphia

Colonial America's finest city was Philadelphia, as traveler Andrew Burnaby noted in his book Travels Through the Middle Settlements in North America in the Years 1759 and 1760:

[Philadelphia] must certainly be the object of every one's wonder and admiration. It is situated upon a tongue of land, a few miles above the confluence of the Delaware and Schuilkill; and contains about 3,000 houses, and 18 or 20,000 inhabitants. It is built north and south upon the banks of the Delaware; and is nearly two miles in length, and three quarters of one in breadth. The streets are laid out with great regularity in parallel lines, intersected by others at right angles, and are handsomely built: on each side there is a pavement of broad stones for [pedestrians]: and in most of them a causeway in the middle for carriages. Upon dark nights it is well lighted, and watched by a patrole: there are many fair houses and public edifices in it. . . . The city is in a vary flourishing state, and inhabited by merchants, artists, tradesmen, and persons of all occupations.

Quoted in Rebecca Brooks Gruver, An American History, *4th ed. New York: Knopf, 1985, p. 64.*

God's Judgment Day was close at hand. Enthralled by Whitefield's raucous sermons, congregations laughed, sang, and screamed with joy. Some collapsed and lay writhing on the floor, believing they were in the presence of God's holy spirit. Known as the Great Awakening, this emotionally charged form of worship spread across the colonies and unintentionally helped prepare isolated American communities for rebellion. Writes British author Paul Johnson, "The Great Awakening's impact altered this separateness. It taught different colonies, tidewaters and piedmonts, coast and up country, to grasp and appreciate what they had in common, which was a very great deal."[5] It was also America's first mass movement, which may have helped set the stage for the coming rebellion against political authorities in England.

The Growth of Education in America

Religion also made an impact on American education. Teachers at most grammar schools in the New England and Middle Colonies taught Protestant religious beliefs along with the classics and basic academic skills. In 1647 the Massachusetts General Court produced "Old Deluder Laws," which required communities to provide education for children to protect their minds from the powers of Satan—also known as the Old Deluder.

In addition, many early colonial universities started as religious institutions. Puritans founded Harvard to make sure their congregations would have educated preachers. Yale was started for the same

reason in Connecticut in 1701. In 1746 Presbyterians created Princeton, and Baptists founded Brown University in 1764; Rutgers was the work of the Dutch Reform Church. In New York the Church of England was the benefactor of King's College, now known as Columbia.

Because Americans lived in a new environment, they quickly discovered that the new knowledge they acquired might be more useful than what was taught in European schools. This discovery gave way to skepticism of those who professed expert academic knowledge, particularly if it was based on ancient, scholarly teachings. American Thought "was a way of thinking pervaded by doubt that the professional thinker could think better than others,"[6] writes historian Daniel Boorstin. As such, reading and self-education were widely practiced arts in the colonies. According to author David McCullough, the eighteenth century in colonial America was, "A day and age that saw no reason why one could not learn whatever was required—learn virtually anything—by the close study of books."[7]

The Impact of the Enlightenment

The American mind was also shaped by the Enlightenment—an ongoing philosophical school of thought that championed the use of reason and respect for human dignity as a guide to creating a more humane and better-functioning society. The Enlightenment also stressed the need for governments to respect and defend individual rights and the importance of putting restraints on political power and public officials gaining approval from those they govern. Enlightenment writers attacked superstition and unquestioning belief in religious traditions. They also expressed skepticism over a criminal justice system that relied on torture, monarchs who claimed they ruled by divine right, and the powerful influence of organized religion on government. One of the most influential writers, British philosopher John Locke, asserted that all human beings were by their birthright entitled to "natural rights" that no other person could deny. Locke and others advanced the notion that a government had the authority to rule only if those being governed gave their consent. Americans were also impressed with the ideas of Charles de Montesquieu, an Enlightenment author and French jurist, who believed that separation of powers helped prevent abuse of government power and protect civil liberties.

Eventually, many of these ideas inspired Americans to revolt against England and to form a new nation based on the U.S. Constitution. Meanwhile, England imposed its authority over the colonies.

American inventor, author, scientist, and statesman Benjamin Franklin learned this authority was unyielding when he traveled to London in the 1750s. As a member of the Pennsylvania Assembly, he was told by Earl Granville, lord president of the council, that, "The King in Council is legislator for the Colonies, and when His Majesty's instructions come there, they are the law of the land."[8] Franklin responded,

> I told him this was new doctrine to me. I had always understood from our charters that our laws were to be made by our assemblies to be presented indeed to the King for his royal assent, but that being once given the King could not repeal or alter them. And as our assemblies could not make permanent laws without his assent, [so] neither could he make a law for them without theirs.[9]

To this Granville assured Franklin that he was very mistaken.

This disagreement only added to the growing rift between the colonists and the British. The division grew wider when England and France went to war in 1754.

John Locke believed that all humans were entitled to certain "natural rights."

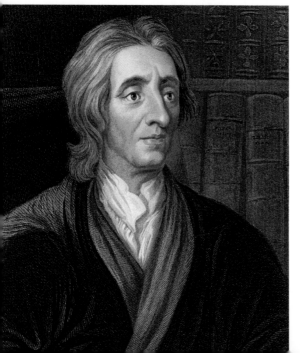

Chapter Two

A Growing Rift

The fighting between England and France was part of a series of wars between the two countries for control of Europe and colonial supremacy around the world that began in 1689. In 1754 the fighting spread to North America where it was called the French and Indian War. At stake was control of the Ohio River Valley, a region coveted by both nations.

When the war began, the colonies sent representatives to meet with one hundred fifty Iroquois leaders in Albany, New York, to work out a mutual defense agreement against the French. It was the first time that the colonies had attempted to create a unified front of any kind. Instead of coming together, however, the delegates bickered and failed to agree on a plan. Their failure disappointed many colonial leaders who realized the importance of the colonies banding together. One of them was Franklin, who believed an effective "Albany Plan" could have

prevented the American Revolution. He clung to this belief even when he was an old man in his eighties, saying, "The colonies so united would have been sufficiently strong to have defended themselves. There would then have been no need of troops from England; of course the . . . [follow-up reasons] for taxing America, and the bloody contest it occasioned, would have been avoided."[10]

The lack of a colonial confederacy, however, did not stop British and colonial armies from overcoming their enemy and capturing the French fortress Québec in Canada. According to the provisions of the 1763 treaty that ended the war, France handed Canada over to Britain along with all French territory east of the Mississippi River. Because France wanted to reward Spain for its help during the war it had given Spain the city of New Orleans plus all French lands west of the Mississippi River. Spain had to cede Florida to the British.

A battle scene from the French and Indian War. Both nations wanted control of the Ohio River Valley.

Since France was now finished as a dominant force in the New World, England was free to push forward with its territorial ambitions. Little stood in the way of the most powerful empire in the world that now enjoyed a commercial and military presence from the Far East to the New World.

British euphoria, however, was tempered by a host of new problems. It soon became apparent that the war had divided, rather than united, Americans and the British. Resentment ran high among many colonists who did not want to fight in a British war. For their part, London officials were offended that so few Americans had fought. In fact, Massachusetts, Connecticut, and New York provided most of the American troops, while other colonies contributed few or none at all.

The war had also doubled the British national debt, which Americans were not eager to help finance. Explains historian Francis D. Cogliano, "In 1763, the average Briton paid 26 shillings per annum in taxes whilst a Massachusetts taxpayer

Colonists Reject the Stamp Act

After the British parliament passed the Stamp Act, angry American delegates from the colonies met in New York in 1765 where they created a document entitled "A Declaration of Rights and Grievances" to express their objections. Many of their assertions appear in the following passage:

The members of this Congress . . . esteem it our indispensable duty to make the following declarations. . . .

> 1st. That his majesty's subjects in these colonies owe the same allegiance to the crown of Great Britain, that is owing from his subjects born with in the realm. . . .

> 2d. That his majesty's subjects in these colonies are entitled to all the inherent rights and privileges of his natural born subjects within the kingdom of Great Britain.

> 3d. No taxes should be imposed on them, but with their own consent, given personally, or by their representatives.

> 4th. That these people of these colonies are not, and . . . [because of their location] cannot be, represented in the House of Commons in Great Britain.

> 5th. That the only representatives of the people of the colonies, are persons . . . [of their own choosing] . . . and that no taxes ever have been, or can be constitutionally imposed on them, but by their respective legislatures. . . .

> 8th. That the late act of parliament . . . [the Stamp Act] . . . [and other acts] . . . [tend to undermine] . . . the rights and liberties of the colonists. . . .

> Lastly, That it is the indispensable duty of these colonies . . . to procure the repeal of the [Stamp Act and other acts that restrict] . . . American commerce.

Readings in World History. Orlando: Harcourt Brace Jovanovich, 1990. pp. 129-30.

contributed one shilling each year to imperial coffers. Americans, British officials concluded, benefited from the protection afforded by the British army and Royal Navy, and it would only be fair if they contributed to their own defense."[11]

The colonies, however, suffered an economic depression following the war and found British demands for money oppressive. In addition, many colonists still smarted from the British wartime practice of quartering, that required the colonies to feed and shelter British troops in barracks (a later quartering act required the use of homes). Anger also united many colonists who felt that British officers and England's upper classes treated Americans as inferiors.

British officials had their own complaints. Outraged that Boston merchants had traded with the Spanish and French in the West Indies during the war, Parliament armed British customs officers with writs of assistance—a type of search warrant—that allowed them to inspect Boston warehouses and ships for contraband.

Authorities in London were also annoyed by relentless American westward expansion into Native American lands. This migration was a clear violation of the Royal Proclamation of October 1763, which stipulated that lands west of the Appalachian Mountains were off limits to further settlement. British policy makers wanted this territory reserved for Native American tribes who were pressured by American encroachment.

Americans and the British also disagreed over how to pay for a military defense against Indian uprisings that resulted when settlers trespassed on Native American lands. British policy makers noted that when Ottawa chief Pontiac led a failed Native American insurrection in the Ohio River Valley, no colonies sent troops to assist settlers and British forts under attack. British officials gave the colonists a choice: Raise patrols for their own protection, or pay through taxation for ten thousand British soldiers to get the job done.

Imposing New Taxes

When the colonies refused to cooperate, Parliament imposed the Sugar Act of 1764 to raise funds for British troops. This measure required that colonists pay a tax on imported sugar as well as other commodities such as coffee, wine, indigo, and woven cloth. The act also denied any violators of the new tax a jury trial and instead gave judges the sole authority to decide their fate.

One year later Parliament passed the Stamp Act, a measure that imposed a tax by requiring a stamp to be purchased and placed on every document, license, bond, or publication in the thirteen colonies. Making matters worse, the British insisted that the tax be paid in coin and not the paper money that the colonies had issued as legal tender. The push for this came from British businessmen who feared that American paper money had decreased in value because the colonies had issued too much of it. This refusal to accept paper money, however, placed a great burden on Americans, who had little gold and silver.

Americans were infuriated that they were expected to pay British taxes with a decreasing money supply. Many British officials, meanwhile, were puzzled by the resentment in the colonies. After all, as historian Thomas Fleming notes, "The Americans of 1776 had the highest standard of living and the lowest taxes in the Western World."[12] But another force also fueled colonial anger: the widespread conviction that the British government denied the colonies the right to elect their own representatives in Parliament.

British officials scoffed at the suggestion that Americans felt deprived. They pointed out that because of property requirements less than 5 percent of all citizens in the British Isles were qualified to vote. Besides, they added, Americans were represented in London because British lawmakers spoke for everyone in the British Empire.

The Sons of Liberty, a radical group of protesters, was led by Sam Adams.

Violent Opposition

These explanations did nothing to quell a gathering storm in the colonies. When summer came, Boston, a city with a history of unrest, erupted with violence. Among the instigators was a secretive and radical group of protesters called the Sons of Liberty, led by brewery owner Sam Adams. Whenever they could, the Sons of Liberty destroyed the hated stamps, and tarred and feathered agents who attempted to collect the tax.

More than just tax anger may have been underway. Historian Howard Zinn suggests that an increasing resentment among the poor and working classes in the colonies against the rich and powerful also played a role in the uprising. Writes Zinn, "In Boston, the economic grievances of the lowest classes mingled with anger against the British and exploded in violence. The leaders of the Independence movement wanted to use that mob energy against England, but also to contain it so that it would not demand too much from them."[13]

Angry mobs riot in protest of the Stamp Act. This event was also known as the Boston Massacre.

Angry mobs also attacked the houses of local tax collectors and colonial officials. One witness to the violence was General Thomas Gage, commander of the British forces in North America: "The Boston Mob . . . attacked, robbed, and destroyed several Houses, and amongst others, that of the Lieutenant Governor. . . . People then began to be terrified at the Spirit they had raised . . . and each individual feared he might be the next Victim to their Rapacity. The same Fears spread thro' the other Provinces."[14]

Violence was not the only reaction to the new tax. Twelve of the thirteen colonies also sent representatives to New York in October 1765 to attend a Stamp Act Congress in June. Here, the delegates denounced the taxes and agreed to boycott all British goods.

Shocked by these strong responses, Parliament repealed the tax in early 1766. However, it also passed the Declaratory Act that made clear in no uncertain terms to Americans that England alone had the right to govern the colonies.

Colonists Reach a Breaking Point

More troubles soon hit the colonies. Charles Townshend, the British chancellor of the exchequer, believed Parliament had been too lenient with the Americans and had not done enough to quell the growing rebelliousness in the colonies. So he led the legislative effort to suspend the New York Assembly for violating the Quartering Act of 1764 requiring Americans to provide living quarters for British troops. In addition, to the amazement of Americans, Parliament imposed new taxes in June 1767 on the colonial importation of lead, paper, and tea to fund British troops in the colonies.

Previously, the colonies lacked a strong feeling of unity. "There was no American nationalism or separatist feeling [from British control],"[15] writes historian Samuel Eliot Morison. In fact, on several occasions the British government had "intervened to protect minority groups against majorities—Quakers and Anglicans in New England against the dominant Puritans, Delaware against Maryland—Georgia against South Carolina."[16]

Now, however, fierce opposition to the so-called "Townshend Acts" united the

Charles Townshend, the British chancellor of the exchequer, made efforts to suspend the New York Assembly for violating the Quartering Act.

colonies together as never before. Angry protestors wrote editorials and pamphlets denouncing the British actions. Suspicion ran high that authorities in London intended to suppress the colonies. Colonists formed various patriot groups called committees of correspondence to provide a network of communications to report any British violations of their rights. In addition, colonial leaders once again called for economic boycotts of British goods.

As anger grew in the colonies, British troops arrived in Boston to keep the peace. For the next year, redcoats—as British troops were called—and local patriots glared at one another on the streets. Finally, tensions snapped on March 5, 1770, when a small group of Bostonians—many of whom were angered by British attempts to force Americans into naval service—heaved snowballs at British soldiers and provoked a volley of gunfire that resulted in the death of several Americans. Although the British commander and six of his men later were acquitted of murder charges, local radicals exaggerated the tragedy in pamphlets as the "Boston Massacre" to encourage further unrest in the colonies.

By now many London officials realized that by passing the Townshend Acts Parliament had blundered. For one thing, British trade had dropped off as a result of British colonial policies. Hostility, rather than obedience, was also widespread across the colonies. Though there was strong support for reversing the latest acts, Parliament did not want to appear cowed by the colonies. To save face,

The Gaspee *was attacked by American colonists after it ran aground in Rhode Island.*

John Adams Confides in His Wife

Both a leader of the American Revolution and a future U.S. president, John Adams often confided to his wife Abigail his impressions of the great events he experienced. The following letter, "John Adams to Abigail Adams, June 17 [1775]" is found in Letters of Delegates to Congress *at the Library of Congress American Memory: Primary Documents in American History.*

I can now inform you that the Congress have made Choice of the modest and virtuous, the amiable, generous and brave George Washington Esqr., to be the General of the American Army, and that he is to repair as soon as possible to the Camp before Boston.(1) This Appointment will have a great Effect, in cementing and securing the Union of these Colonies. The Continent is really in earnest in defending the Country. They have voted Ten Companies of Rifle Men to be sent from Pennsylvania, Maryland and Virginia, to join the Army before Boston.(2) These are an excellent Species of Light Infantry. They use a peculiar Kind of . . . Rifle—it has . . . Grooves within the Barrell, and carries [fires] a Ball, with great Exactness to great Distances. They are the most accurate Marksmen in the World. I begin to hope We shall not sit all Summer.

I hope the People of our Province, will treat the General with all that Confidence and Affection, that Politeness and Respect, which is due to one of the most important Characters in the World. The Liberties of America, depend upon him, in a great Degree.

My Duty to your Uncle Quincy—your Papa, Mama and mine—my Brothers and sisters and yours. Adieu.

"John Adams to Abigail Adams, June 17 [1775]," *Letters of Delegates to Congress 1774–1789, vol. 1, August 1774–August 1775*, p. 498.

Lord North, the new British chancellor of the exchequer, persuaded Parliament to repeal all recent measures taken against America except the tax on tea.

North's actions brought a period of calm. It was shattered, however, on June 9, 1772, when the British vessel *Gaspee* ran aground searching for smugglers in Narragansett Bay, off Rhode Island. That night a group of men from Providence boarded the ship, burned it, and shot the captain. A commission dispatched by the British government investigated the matter but uncovered no suspects when local people refused to cooperate.

The Boston Tea Party

Relations between the colonies and England worsened a year later when the East India Company—a British trading

A mob of Boston men revolted against a tax on tea by throwing tea from English ships into Boston Harbor. This was known as the Boston Tea Party.

company operating in India—tried to avoid economic ruin. Parliament sought to help the company by allowing it to bypass colonial merchants and sell tea directly to Americans. Though the price of tea dropped for consumers, American businessmen lost money. Meanwhile, the British also insisted on collecting a tax on tea—one that they had ignored for many years.

Another tax revolt soon materialized. On December 16, 1773, a mob of about two thousand Boston men dressed as Mohawk Indians boarded ships in the Boston harbor and dumped 345 crates of British tea into the sea. Other protests broke out in Charleston, New York, and Philadelphia.

News of the "Boston Tea Party" outraged Parliament. It retaliated by closing the port of Boston and threatening to keep it sealed under military rule until the colonists paid for the ruined tea, which today would be worth about $1 million. As extra punishment, the British government reduced the powers of the colonial representative assemblies and increased the powers of colonial governors. Parliament also decreed that any royal officers accused of murder would stand trial in London, not America. Finally, British officials extended the southern border of Québec, Canada—an area typified by French culture but dominated by British rule—to the Ohio River.

Not only did this blunt American expansion, it also made many Americans fear encroaching French attitudes regarding religion and government. Parliament also imposed a new Quartering Act that required Americans to provide shelter for British troops within their own homes and hotels, not barracks.

Bostonians were not the only Americans outraged by these actions. Infuriated leaders from most of the other colonies sent delegates to a hastily called meeting of the Continental Congress in Philadelphia in September 1774. Here, fiery speakers denounced England's punitive "Intolerable Acts" and urged all Americans to boycott all British imports and exports. A year earlier, the congress declared that the British had no right to tax the colonies. Now a growing number of delegates went further by arguing that Parliament had no authority over the colonies whatsoever. Radicals, however, failed to convince the congress to break all ties with England.

Eyewitness to the Boston Massacre

On March 5, 1770, a hostile crowd of Bostonians confronted a unit of eight British soldiers. The harassed soldiers opened fire on the Bostonians, wounding six and killing five. They were later arrested and charged with murder. Captain Thomas Preston, the officer in charge, provided the following eyewitness account of the event. At the conclusion of his trial, Preston was acquitted.

About 9 [o'clock] some of the guard came to and informed me the town inhabitants were assembling to attack the troops. . . . [A]fter I reached the guard, about 100 people passed in and went toward the custom house where the king's money is lodged. They immediately surrounded the sentry posted there, and with clubs and other weapons threatened to execute their vengeance on him. I was soon informed by a townsman their intention was to carry off the soldier from his post and probably murder him. . . . The mob still increased and [was] more outrageous, striking their clubs or bludgeons one against another, and calling out come on you rascals, you bloody backs, you lobster scoundrels, fire if you dare, . . . [O]ne of the soldiers having received a severe blow with a stick, stepped a little on one side and instantly fired, on which turning to ask him why he fired without orders, I was struck with a club on my arm, which for some time deprived me of the use of it. . . . [A] general attack was made on the men by a great number of heavy clubs and snow-balls being thrown at them, by which all our lives were in imminent dangers.

Quoted in Steven C. Bullock, *The American Revolution: A History in Documents.* New York: Oxford University Press, pp. 31–34.

American militiamen confront British troops at the Battle of Lexington.

Most delegates were not ready for such a drastic move. Instead, they devised a compromise resolution that recognized only England's right to regulate trade to pay for naval protection of American ships.

North and his allies in Parliament, however, rejected the Continental Congress's compromise and passed new measures that excluded New Englanders from fishing off the coast of Newfoundland and banned them from trading anywhere except England and the West Indies. In addition, Parliament cut off shipments of weapons to the colonies.

General Gage Reacts

Though many in Parliament now expected war, they mistakenly believed that their enemy was limited to rebels in Massachusetts. General Thomas Gage, now the governor of Massachusetts, knew better and sent warnings to London that all the colonies were prepared to fight. He also insisted that he needed twenty thousand troops to put down the rising rebellion. King George III, however, dismissed Gage's concerns and sent only thirty-five hundred men.

By April 1775 informers had alerted Gage that colonial patriots were stockpiling guns and ammunition at Concord, a town outside Boston. Soon seven hundred British redcoats marched to seize the hidden war materials. Before dawn, horseback riders, including the famous Paul Revere, galloped across the countryside, accompanied by the sounds of church bells and cannon fire alerting the local militia that British troops were on the move.

Armed militiamen confronted British troops as they rode through the town of Lexington. Shots rang out, sparking a gun battle. Moments later eight Americans lay dead, and Gage's men hurried on to Concord. Along the way, militiamen harassed them with hit-and-run tactics.

By the time the fighting ended, the British had suffered more than 270 casualties; the Americans suffered 88. The Revolution had begun.

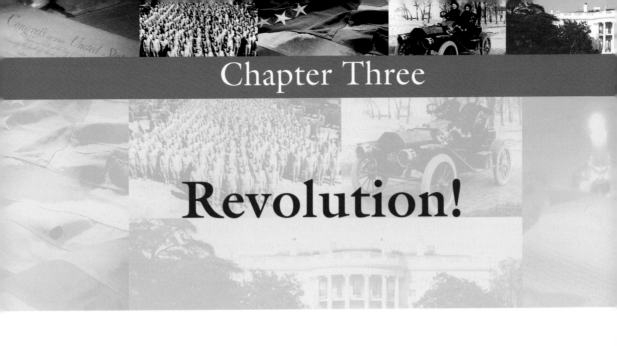

Chapter Three

Revolution!

As news of the bloodshed in Massachusetts spread, royal authority collapsed across the colonies. Growing numbers of Americans took up arms and allied themselves with the rebels. Other Americans who remained loyal to England, however, were horrified by the growing rebellion and fled to the protection of British troops or even left the colonies.

Ethan Allen confronts the sleepy British commander of Fort Ticonderoga. Allen's Vermont Green Mountain Boys seized the fort in May 1775.

When colonial assemblies now met, they did so as independent governments—not as entities of the British Crown—and prepared for conflict. War was also on the minds of the delegates who arrived in Philadelphia on May 10, 1775, for the Second Continental Congress. Fighting continued in Boston. In addition, American forces led by Ethan Allen and a militia group he organized called the Vermont Green Mountain Boys had that very day occupied Fort Ticonderoga, New York, and seized British cannons. Under the supervision of a Boston bookseller, Henry Knox, American troops transported the weapons across mountains and rivers to help George Washington, whose forces waited outside of Boston. Shaken by the ongoing violence, the delegates created America's first independent centralized government. One of the new government's first official acts was to take charge of the militia forces fighting in Massachusetts and put them under the command of a tall, stately Virginian, General George Washington, whose larger task was to turn the volunteers into a disciplined army. Though a widely trusted military leader, Washington insisted that he was not qualified for the position, as he made clear in an acceptance speech addressed to John Hancock of Massachusetts during a session of the congress:

I am truly sensible of the high honor done me in this appointment, yet I feel great distress from a consciousness that my abilities and military experience may not be equal to the extensive and important trust. However, as the Congress desire it, I will enter upon the momentous duty and exert every power I possess in the service and for the support of the glorious Cause . . . [yet] . . . I do not think myself equal to the command I [am] honored with.[17]

The delegates voted to support Washington's troops with

George Washington was placed in charge of the militia forces fighting in Massachusetts.

A British Officer Proclaims Support for the King's Crackdown on the Colonists

Following the outbreak of fighting in America, Parliament hastily convened on July 26, 1775, to debate how the British government should respond. John Dyke Acland of Devonshire, a young army officer, offered this support of his country's action:

L et me remind you of those extensive and successful wars that this country has carried on before the continent of America was known. Let me turn your attention to that period when you defended this very people from the attacks of the most powerful and valiant nation in Europe [France], when your armies gave law, and your fleets rode triumphant on every coast. Shall we be told then that this people [the Americans], whose greatness is the work of our hands, and whose insolence [disrespect] arises from our divisions, who have mistaken the lenity of this country for its weakness, and the reluctance to punish, for a want [lack] of power to vindicate the violated rights of British subjects—shall we be told that such a people can resist the powerful efforts of this nation?

Quoted in David McCullough, *1776*. New York: Simon & Schuster, 2005, p. 14.

paper money, and turned to other urgent issues. By now radicals in the congress demanded an immediate break with England, but once again many other delegates were reluctant to sever all ties with England. These conservatives were still loyal to the king despite their grievances with Parliament. In July the congress reached a compromise and voted to petition the king to rescue the colonies from troubles caused by his members of Parliament. The congress also prepared a document that claimed that the tyranny of Parliament had left the congress no choice but to take up arms to protect their property, a move that Americans would willingly put aside once their rights were recognized: "[W]e mean not to dissolve that union which has so long and so happily subsisted between us, and which we sincerely wish to see restored."[18]

George III and North, however, were unmoved; they saw only treason at work in the colonies, and dispatched twenty-five thousand more troops to America to crush all rebels. In addition, Parliament cut off all trade with the colonies and authorized British vessels to intercept American merchant ships and search for contraband.

Meanwhile, the fighting spread. In June, British regulars under General William Howe drove armed militiamen from Breed's Hill near Boston after the Americans ran out of gunpowder. Next, about a thousand Americans plunged into Canada to prevent a British attack from the north. Led by General Richard Montgomery and Colonel Benedict Arnold, the patriots—as the American fighters were now called—captured Montreal but failed to occupy Québec due to the effects of smallpox, hunger and freezing weather. Compounding these woes was Canada's failure to accept an American invitation to fight the British.

During the next few months the Continental Congress established the first American navy, which—along with the arrival of the cannons from Ft. Ticonderoga—helped to force the evacuation of the British from Boston on March 17, 1776. Three months later British warships were turned back after bombarding a fort made of palm trees near Charleston, South Carolina.

Paine Inspires Patriots

By now a growing number of Americans, including many who had previously opposed war, supported the call for independence. Increasingly, colonists found inspiration from the arguments of a popular new pamphlet called *Common Sense* that first appeared in January 1776. The author was Thomas Paine, a young Englishman who, despite having lived in America for only the past two years, ardently championed the American cause. Using fiery, passionate, and compelling words, Paine implored readers to reject a king willing to ignore their rights and even kill them. Moreover, he asserted, England was no longer fit to govern America. "There is something absurd in supposing a continent to be perpetually governed by an island,"[19] wrote Paine. Americans, he insisted, should fight for their independence, an idea that was sweeping across the colonies like wildfire.

Paine's words proved intoxicating to Americans at all levels. John Adams, a leader in the Revolution and a future U.S. president observed, "History will ascribe the [American] Revolution to Thomas Paine. . . . Without the pen of Paine, the sword of Washington would have been wielded in vain."[20]

Thomas Paine provided inspiration to Americans through his Common Sense *pamphlet.*

Thomas Paine's *Common Sense* Stirs Patriots

Few documents inspired Americans to fight for independence as the sixteen pamphlets written by Thomas Paine entitled The American Crisis *and signed "Common Sense"—which became the namesake for the series. The following segment, which comes from Part III of Common Sense, focuses on Paine's concluding reasons why America should separate from Great Britain:*

[T]he] most powerful of all arguments is, that nothing but independence, i.e. a continental form of government, can keep the peace of the continent and preserve it inviolate [secure] from civil wars. I dread the event of a reconciliation [compromise] with Britain *now*, as it is more than probable that it will be followed by a revolt somewhere or other, the consequences of which may be far more fatal than all the malice of Britain.

[T]he general temper of the colonies towards a British government will be like that of a youth who is nearly out of his time; they will care very little about her. And a government which cannot preserve the peace is no government at all, and in that case we pay our money for nothing; and pray what is it that Britain can do, whose power will be wholly on paper, should a civil tumult break out the very day after reconciliation? I have heard some men say, many of whom I believe spoke without thinking, that they dreaded an independence, fearing that it would produce civil wars. It is but seldom that our first thoughts are truly correct, and that is the case here; for there is ten times more to dread from a patched up connection than from independence. I make the sufferer's case my own, and I protest, that were I driven from house and home, my property destroyed, and my circumstances ruined, that as a man, sensible of injuries, I could never relish the doctrine of reconciliation, or consider myself bound thereby.

Quoted in Sculley Bradley et. al, eds., *The American Tradition in Literature.* New York: Norton, 1967, pp. 293–94.

As the battle cry of freedom spread through the colonies, any hopes of reconciliation with England disappeared in the Second Continental Congress. Almost all its members on the patriot side now agreed with Richard Henry Lee of the Virginia delegation, who on June 7, 1776, moved that "These united colonies are, and ought to be, free and independent states."[21]

Jefferson Authors the Declaration of Independence

On July 2 the congress officially voted in favor of independence from England.

can write ten times better than I can."[22]

With editing help from Franklin and Adams, Jefferson produced the Declaration of Independence, the world-famous document that artfully expressed many ideas inspired by the Enlightenment, particularly those initially penned by English philosopher John Locke. Neither a law nor constitution, the declaration was instead an open letter that proclaimed the radical idea that a just government depended on the consent of the governed. Moreover, it vowed "All men are created equal" and "endowed by their Creator with certain unalienable rights." When a government no longer served the needs of the people, wrote Jefferson, those same people had a right to abolish the government and establish a new one. In addition, the declaration contained a long list of grievances against the king.

The Declaration Becomes Official

On July 4 the congress officially adopted the declaration, though individual members signed it over a period of months. Such a move made clear to the world what the patriots wanted. It also provided the colonies with an unmistakable purpose to

Delegates then chose a committee to put ideas into writing. The man selected by the committee to compose the document was Thomas Jefferson of Virginia—a farmer, scholar, writer, inventor, and proponent of independence. Jefferson wondered aloud why he was picked.

Delegate John Adams replied, "Reason first, you are a Virginian, and a Virginian ought to appear at the head of this business. Reason second, I am obnoxious, suspected, and unpopular. You are very much otherwise. Reason third, you

guide them through the dark days ahead. It also meant that Washington's troops were no longer fighting to preserve their rights as Englishmen; now they were fighting for independence. To British loyalists such a break was treasonous, a sentiment those at the signing of the Declaration of Independence well understood. John Hancock of Massachusetts urged all delegates to write their names on the dangerous document to express unity. "We must hang together,"[23] he said. Reportedly, Franklin replied, "Yes, we must all hang together, or most assuredly, we shall all hang separately."[24]

By the next day, horseback riders headed to all thirteen states to deliver copies of the Declaration of Independence. When the declaration was read aloud to a public gathering five days later in Philadelphia, militiamen and townspeople cheered. Some knocked down a lead statue of George III from a prominent place in town.

Not all Americans, however, supported revolution. Adams suggested that perhaps a third of the population remained loyal to the Crown, though many of these supporters fled the colonies when fighting broke out. Another third was indifferent to politics, and a final third favored independence. Though lacking a majority, patriots nonetheless had enough supporters to keep the independence movement going.

A Rebel Doctor's First Experience of the Horrors of War

In the following passage Dr. Benjamin Rush, a signer of the Declaration of Independence, records his shock at his first glimpse of the gore of war:

The American army retired and left the British in possession of Trenton. The scene which accompanied and followed this combat was new to me. The first wounded man that came off the field was a New England soldier. His right hand hung a little above his wrist by nothing but a piece of skin. It had been broken by a cannon ball. I took charge of him and directed him to a house on the river which had been appropriated for a hospital. In the evening all the wounded, about 20 in number, were brought to this hospital and dressed by Dr. [John] Cochran, myself, and several young surgeons who acted under our direction. We all lay down on some straw in the same room with our wounded patients. It was now for the first time war appeared to me in its awful plenitude of horrors. I want [lack] words to describe the anguish of my soul, excited by the cries and groans and convulsions of the men who lay by my side.

Quoted in David McCullough, *1776*. New York: Simon & Schuster, 2005, p. 287.

The Continental Army built winter cabins to protect themselves from the harsh winter. The army faced many difficulties, including exposure to the elements.

Volunteers vs. Regulars

The Continental Army, however, had few resources. Its volunteer soldiers lacked discipline, organization, and military tradition. Life was hard and dangerous. Disease, hunger, infection, boredom, isolation, and exposure to the elements were the soldiers' constant companions. Lack of support from their fellow Americans was another problem. Even the congress could forsake them, as George Washington all too often found out when he had to beg for money and supplies for his troops. Low pay and no compensation for war injuries undermined the morale of the American fighting force.

Patriot soldiers faced a professional army of British regulars and German mercenaries, backed by the most powerful empire on earth. Unlike the Americans, the British troops were experienced and well supplied.

The colonists, however, enjoyed a few advantages. Although their militias were spread out over vast areas, the American fighters knew well the terrain they fought upon. Americans also had a long tradition of bearing arms and defending themselves from Native Americans and other enemies. Drawing upon these experiences, they waged guerrilla war upon the British with a newly designed gun, equipped with rifling in the barrels that made their weapons more accurate. Several highly competent officers also commanded the American troops. The greatest of them was Washington, who commanded respect from revolutionary-era Americans.

Many Americans soldiers, roused by the cry of independence, also had a great will to win. Finally, American colonists now had a government—though a deeply flawed one—that legitimized their grievances against the king and compellingly argued that they had a legal right to resist British tyranny.

The Revolution Divides the British People

Many people in Britain, including several members in Parliament, sympathized with the American cause and opposed the use of violence against them. Some believed the Americans were at war with the king and the British government, not the British people. Others were convinced the war in America was futile and would end disastrously. An ailing British statesman, William Pitt, warned Parliament in 1777, "You may ravage—you cannot conquer; it is impossible; you cannot conquer the Americans; I might as well talk of driving them before me with this crutch."[25]

Many nobles also opposed the king's war efforts. Even before the fighting in America had begun, these aristocrats were at odds with George III's attempts to revive the power of the monarchy that had been weakened in previous years. Though the nobility had few qualms over exploiting the colonies themselves, they did not want the king to strengthen his position as a war leader at their own political expense.

Because of mounting domestic opposition to the war, the British government had to employ German mercenaries called Hessians when it was unable to enlist enough British soldiers to fight.

The Crown Escalates the Fighting

Such concerns, however, did not curb the king's desire to wage war. In response to

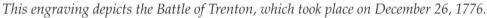

This engraving depicts the Battle of Trenton, which took place on December 26, 1776.

the Declaration of Independence, North, acting on the king's behalf, escalated the war by dispatching 45,000 British troops and 30,000 Hessians to America. A large British fleet soon appeared in New York Harbor. Within weeks Royal troops were battling 23,000 experienced American fighters.

By September, however, having endured fierce fighting, the tattered patriots evacuated and were chased across Manhattan. Two months later Washington's forces retreated across New Jersey, pursued by Howe's redcoats. During the chase Howe sent a portion of his troops into Rhode Island, where they took over the city of Newport on December 8.

Meanwhile, Washington's troops had crossed the Delaware River into Pennsylvania, destroying bridges behind them. Safely camped on the other side, they waited as winter settled in. The situation was grim for the Americans. By now Washington's forces numbered only about eight thousand—all of them hungry, cold, dejected, and dressed in rags. Soon, almost three-fourths of them would complete their enlistments and be eligible to go home. Faced with this reality, Washington decided to use his troops while he still had men to command.

On the night of December 25, 1776, Washington and his troops huddled in small boats as they crossed the Delaware River in freezing rain. Just before dawn they attacked sleeping Hessian troops in Trenton, New Jersey, killing their commander and capturing 990 soldiers. Incredibly, the Americans lost only four men.

Buoyed by this major success, many of Washington's men stayed with the general as he led another attack against British redcoats at Princeton two weeks later, forcing them to retreat to New Brunswick, Canada. Afterward, the fatigued Americans settled in at Morristown and waited for spring.

A Turning Point

Warm weather brought renewed fighting. In September Howe's forces fended off attacks from Washington's men and captured Philadelphia, a stronghold of patriots. Howe was triumphant again a week later at Germanton when his men repelled another attack from Washington.

Things ended badly, however, for another British commander, General "Gentleman Johnny" Burgoyne who, accompanied by his mistress and thirty carts carrying his personal belongings, led more than seven thousand men from Fort St. Johns in Canada to take control of the Hudson River in New York. But Burgoyne underestimated the tenacity of the patriots waiting for him. On October 17, 1777, American forces led by General Horatio Gates and Arnold overwhelmed Burgoyne's army, forcing his surrender at Freeman's Farm in Saratoga.

This American victory proved to be a turning point in the war. For one thing, American morale soared when the colonists discovered that they could defeat and capture a British army. It also perturbed authorities in London, who now feared that the Americans were actually capable of winning the war. Hoping to end hostilities, they informed the

A French Volunteer Describes the Misery of Valley Forge

A French volunteer known as the Chevalier de Pontgibaud traveled to the American encampment at Valley Forge in the winter of 1777. In the following passage he describes the wretched conditions he found there:

Soon I came in sight of the camp. My imagination had pictured an army with uniforms, the glitter of arms standards, etc., in short, military pomp of all sorts. Instead . . . I saw, grouped together or standing alone, a few militiamen, poorly clad, and for the most part without shoes—many of them badly armed, but all well supplied with provisions. . . . In passing through the camp I also noticed soldiers wearing cotton nightcaps under their hats, and some having for cloaks or greatcoats, coarse woolen blankets, exactly like those provided for the patients in our French hospitals. I learned afterwards that these were the officers and generals.

Such, in strict truth was, at the time I came amongst them the appearance of this armed mob, the leader of whom was the man who has rendered the name of Washington famous; such were the colonists—unskilled warriors who learned in a few years how to conquer the finest troops that England could send against them.

Quoted in Stephen Ambrose and Douglas Brinkley, *Witness to America: An Illustrated Documentary History of the United States from the Revolution to Today.* New York: HarperCollins, 1999, pp. 20–21.

congress that the British government was willing to repeal every unpopular measure enacted since 1763.

The Americans, however, were in no mood for reconciliation. Congress rejected the peace offering and instead turned to England's old enemy, France, which had unofficially supplied the Americans with military and financial help during much of the war.

Until now, France had wavered in lending its full support. After the American triumph at Saratoga, however, French king Louis XVI believed that America could win the war and cost England its American colonies. Because a weakened England was in France's best interest, Louis agreed in February 1778 to make an official military alliance with the Americans and declared war against England. Spain joined France a year later.

Even better news for the patriots came when France gave up new territorial claims of its own in North America and agreed that America alone would lay claim to any British lands obtained through war. These concessions boosted American morale, because for the first time a foreign power had recognized America as an independent nation.

Despite a huge influx of much-needed money, munitions, ships, and manpower

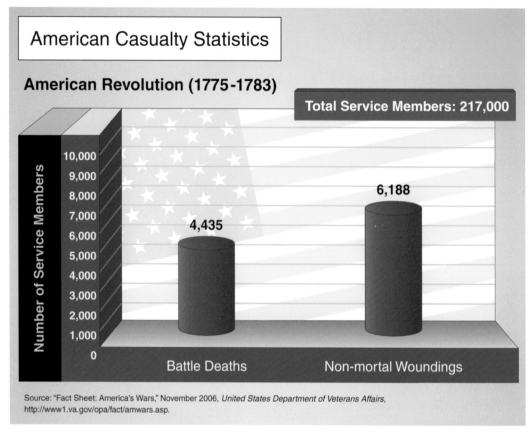

American Casualty Statistics

American Revolution (1775-1783)

Total Service Members: 217,000

Number of Service Members

10,000
9,000
8,000
7,000
6,000
5,000
4,000
3,000
2,000
1,000
0

4,435

Battle Deaths

6,188

Non-mortal Woundings

Source: "Fact Sheet: America's Wars," November 2006, *United States Department of Veterans Affairs*, http://www1.va.gov/opa/fact/amwars.asp.

from France, the war was far from over. Fighting, in fact, lasted three more years, in part because British troops fortified their bases at New York City and Rhode Island, allowing British General Henry Clinton to concentrate on the southern colonies. Here the British expected to find strong pockets of loyalists who would rush to aid England. By the end of the year, the British had taken Savannah and soon controlled all of Georgia. This success allowed the British to again set up royal government in the state.

A year and a half later the redcoats attacked Charleston, South Carolina. After three months of fighting, the South's most important city surrendered in May 1780.

Beginning of the End

The next big campaign took place when British general Charles Cornwallis successfully led his troops into the hills of South Carolina and beat the Americans at the Battle of Camden. From here his men battled their way through North Carolina and into Yorktown, Virginia, where his forces built fortifications along the seacoast and waited for British warships to provide military support.

Meanwhile, American volunteers under the leadership of George Rogers Clark seized a British fort on the Wabash River. In addition, French troops laid siege to Newport and New York City. Soon afterward Washington launched a surprise attack against Cornwallis at Yorktown.

As Washington's troops advanced, a French fleet occupied the Chesapeake River and blocked British ships, thus cutting off supplies to Cornwallis's men and their means of escape. On October 19, 1781, a battered and out-maneuvered Cornwallis had no choice but to hoist up the white flag of surrender. As the British military band played "The World Turned Upside Down," American troops took control of Cornwallis's eight thousand redcoats. Though a few skirmishes continued after Cornwallis's surrender, the war was over.

Aftermath of War

England's defeat caused the fall of North and his ministers, who were replaced by new officials more sympathetic to the American cause. A peace treaty, however, was delayed because France was still at war with England and expected the Americans to wait until hostilities ended before negotiating.

However, the American negotiating team became wary of French intentions and decided to negotiate in secret with their British counterparts. The Americans were pleased to discover that England was eager to offer good terms to drive a wedge between the Americans and the French.

Under the terms of the final treaty, signed in September 1783 and ratified by the congress in January 1784, George III recognized American independence. The treaty also established that America's boundaries ranged from the Atlantic to the Mississippi and from the Great Lakes to Florida. It lifted any British barrier to Americans wanting to

General Cornwallis surrenders to George Washington at Yorktown.

navigate the Mississippi and fish off the coast of Newfoundland. In addition, the British agreed to remove their troops from the new nation as soon as they were able. For their part, American officials promised to urge the states to compensate British loyalists for any confiscated property and to try to remove any legal obstacles to the collection of prewar debts owed to businessmen in England.

At last Americans had achieved independence and recognition as a sovereign nation. War had bound the nation together. Now, however, the nation's leaders faced the daunting task of creating a country that could hold together during a time of peace.

Chapter Four

A Young Republic Struggles to Stay Together

Patriots cheered and hoisted the American flag as British redcoats departed New York City on November 25, 1783. Their joy, however, was tempered by the tragedy of war. Much of the city around them lay in ruins. War had also ravaged other American cities, towns, and villages. Everywhere Americans faced massive reconstruction. Both the national and state governments staggered under enormous war debts. Thousands of families grieved over the dead, and many war veterans struggled with disfigurement, shattered bodies, and psychological trauma.

The new republic consisted of only about 3,250,000 people, excluding Native Americans. Of these, 600,000 were slaves with no rights. Another million or so were women, who if married, had no property rights, could not vote, and could not receive a public education. Another 300,000 were indentured servants. Historian William Miller estimates that

only 400,000 men could call themselves free in the 1780s. And many of them were badly educated, had no property, and therefore no political rights. Miller estimates that only about 120,000 males met the qualifications to vote, and even fewer met higher standards to run for office.

Striving for Equality

Still, patriots rich and poor cared deeply about how they should now live. Their political senses had been stirred by the Revolution. Now freed of British control, Americans asserted their rights, freedoms, goals, and interests. The country was suddenly swept up by the ideals of democracy and equality, as people celebrated the words "All men are created equal" in the Declaration of Independence. Jefferson most likely meant that Americans were equal to the British as citizens; but now his phrase took on a new meaning. Quite suddenly many Americans widened and deepened the

George Washington triumphantly enters New York after the British departed the city.

meaning of equality. Opposition to royalty and privileged classes spawned in the revolutionary period now lingered after the war and fueled the equality movement. State governments also contributed to the trend by outlawing titles of nobility from foreign countries.

The economic impact of war also helped to level the economic disparity of America's social classes. In many cases wealthy merchants suffered financial loss when fighting destroyed their businesses. Others suffered when British blockades prevented American ships from carrying cargo to market. Farmers, however, often saw their fortunes rise by selling vegetables and grain to the military. Meanwhile, state governments confiscated and auctioned the properties of wealthy loyalists who had been driven out of America to live in Canada, the West Indies, or England. Though speculators bought many of these estates, they often sold them as small and affordable parcels of land, enabling many Americans to own property for the first time. At the same time, most states reduced the property requirement to vote, thus expanding the political franchise to poorer people. New laws were also passed that encouraged the dispersion of a deceased person's estate among all heirs, not just the eldest son, as had been the case in England.

Reconsidering Slavery

The equality movement, however, also forced Americans to reconsider slavery. During the Revolutionary War, thousands of blacks had fought for both patriots and the British with hopes of being rewarded with freedom. At the end of

British loyalists were often driven out of America. Their property and wealth was confiscated by the new government.

the war, great numbers departed on British ships to live as free people abroad. Others were left behind and returned to slavery. Now, however, these individuals wanted the same rights implied in the Declaration of Independence. In 1780 seven blacks caught up in the new spirit petitioned the state government of Massachusetts for the right to vote. Following the example set by American revolutionaries, they argued that taxation without representation was unjust: "We . . . [are distressed] . . . that while we are not allowed the Privalage of freemen of the State having no vote or Influence in the Election of those that Tax us yet many of our Colour (as is well known) have cheerfully Entered the field of Battle in the defense of the Common Cause [the American Revolution] and . . . [against England's unfair system of taxation]."[26]

Though some Americans, including southerners, freed their slaves, and northern states began abolishing slavery, the entire country was not yet ready for the emancipation of blacks. In the Deep South, in fact, the institution of slavery continued for another eight decades until the nation erupted in civil war.

A Crisis in Self-Government

How to govern a new nation was the most pressing problem faced by Americans. This became increasingly clear as the spirit of wartime unity faded. In fact, for many the Revolution may have bolstered a love of state, rather than nation.

Overseas, meanwhile, watchful British observers doubted America's ability to become a successful sovereign nation. In fact, because many royal authorities expected the American experiment with independence to fail, they scorned attempts by their former colonies to negotiate fair trade practices. Josiah Tucker, dean of England's Gloucester Cathedral, predicted of the former colonists, "A disunited people till the end of time, suspicious and distrustful of each other, they will be divided and subdivided into little commonwealths or principalities, according to natural boundaries."[27]

Tucker's vision, however, proved false. American state governments, in fact, were managing to govern themselves in the wake of the British departure. State constitutions, bills of rights, and republics created during the Revolution still functioned effectively.

Trouble mounted, however, at the national level. Here, America, as a *nation,* headed toward disunity. Much of the problem lay with the nation's first constitution, the Articles of Confederation, forged by the states during the Revolution, which called for a "league of friendship" between the former colonies. It was now clear, however, in the wake of war, that under this loose federation the states acted as separate republics rather than as one nation. They bickered over taxes and tariffs. New York, for instance, taxed firewood from Connecticut and vegetables from New Jersey. States also imposed taxes on any foreign goods crossing their borders from other states.

Boundary disputes often strained relations between states. According to their charters, Georgia, Virginia, the Carolinas, Connecticut, and Massachusetts could claim territorial western boundaries that reached the Pacific Ocean. All too often these claims clashed and resulted in conflict. Pennsylvania and Virginia came to blows over land in the Pittsburgh area, while settlers in Kentucky threatened to use violence to cause that state to break away from Virginia.

Title page of the Articles of Confederation, which was the nation's first constitution.

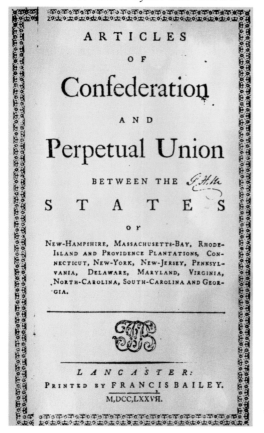

ARTICLES
OF
Confederation
AND
Perpetual Union
BETWEEN THE *G.H.K.*
STATES
OF
NEW-HAMPSHIRE, MASSACHUSETTS-BAY, RHODE-ISLAND AND PROVIDENCE PLANTATIONS, CONNECTICUT, NEW-YORK, NEW-JERSEY, PENNSYLVANIA, DELAWARE, MARYLAND, VIRGINIA, NORTH-CAROLINA, SOUTH-CAROLINA AND GEORGIA.

LANCASTER:
PRINTED BY FRANCIS BAILEY.
M,DCC,LXXVII.

A Doctor Explains How War Changed America

David Ramsay, a South Carolina physician and witness to the American Revolution, observed in his History of the American Revolution, *published in 1789, how the war had changed American society:*

The Americans knew but little of one another previous to the Revolution. Trade and business had brought the inhabitants of their seaports acquainted with each other, but the bulk of the people in the interior country were unacquainted with their fellow citizens. A Continental army and Congress composed of men from all the states, by freely mixing together, were assimilated into one mass. Individuals of both, mingling with the citizens, disseminated [communicated] principles of union [ideas for national unity] among them. Local prejudices abated [lessened].

. . . Intermarriages of different states were much more common than before the war and became an additional cement to the Union. Unreasonable jealousies had existed between the inhabitants of the Eastern and of the Southern states, but on becoming better acquainted with each other, these in a great measure subsided.

. . . Religious bigotry had broken in upon the peace of various sects before the American war. This was kept up by partial establishments, and by a dread that the Church of England . . . would . . . triumph over all other denominations. These apprehensions [worries] were done away by the Revolution.

Quoted in Stephen Ambrose and Douglas Brinkley, *Witness to America: An Illustrated Documentary History of the United States from the Revolution to Today.* New York: HarperCollins, 1999, p. 25.

Meanwhile, Delaware, Maryland, New Jersey, Pennsylvania, and Rhode Island—whose territorial boundaries were fixed by the sea or their neighboring states—wanted the congress to take charge of the western territories, make them possessions of the entire nation, and set up rules for statehood.

Though the congress ultimately conjured up the power to resolve this western boundary issue, other legal problems proved harder, if not impossible, to fix. No longer could states take interstate disputes to British judges. Not much help came from the national government because the Articles of Confederation provided no judiciary. Nor did it make available a permanent executive branch of government.

The Articles of Confederation had many other flaws. Under its provisions, each state had one vote to cast for laws, regardless of the size of its population. Congress was crippled by a provision that some important bills, such as those having to do with treaties and money,

Thomas Jefferson Calls for Unity

In a February 15, 1783, letter to fellow Virginian Edmund Randolph, Jefferson confesses his concern that the new American republic may be headed to war:

I find also the pride of [independence] taking deep and dangerous hold on the hearts of individual states. I know no danger so dreadful and so probable as that of internal contests. And I know no remedy so likely to prevent it as the strengthening the band that connects us. We have substituted a Congress of deputies from every state to perform this task; but we have done nothing which would enable them to enforce their decisions. What will be the case? They will not be enforced. The states will go to war with each other in defiance of Congress; one will call in France to her assistance; and Great Britain, and so we shall have all the wars of Europe brought to our own doors. . . . I feel great comfort on the prospect of getting yourself and two or three others into the legislatures. My humble and earnest prayer to Almighty god will be that you may bring into fashion principles suited to the form of government we have adopted, and not of that we have rejected, that you will first lay your shoulders to strengthening the band of our confederacy and averting those cruel evils to which its present weakness will expose us.

Quoted in John M. Blum, William S. McFeely, Edmund S. Morgan, Arthur M. Schlesinger Jr., Kenneth M. Stampp, and C. Vann Woodward, *The National Experience: A History of the United States*, 6th ed. San Diego: Harcourt Brace Jovanovich, 1985, p. 132.

required a two-thirds majority of votes to pass. Because of this rule, a significant piece of legislation could be defeated even though most delegates supported it. In 1782, for instance, an effort was made to give the congress the right to levy a duty on foreign exports, but Rhode Island refused to go along, and the effort died. As a result the congress lacked the authority to control the supply and prices of goods from foreign countries that hurt American producers and consumers.

Congress was also unable to regulate commerce or impose taxes. Nor could it force states to provide funds to pay the cost of governance. As a result many states refused to pay, angering those states that did. Meanwhile, the national debt grew larger.

Other money matters added to the nation's problems. Each state, for example, coined its own money and printed paper money that inflated the money supply. In addition, now and then people used salt pork, tobacco, and whaling oil as currency instead of money.

Growing Fears and Problems

As the national government appeared to be heading into anarchy, some Americans feared that states might even fight among themselves, break away from the confederacy, and form alliances with Spain, France, or England. A few conservative Americans demanded a monarchy or military rule to keep order in the states.

Trouble from external forces, meanwhile, loomed beyond the western borders of the United States. Spain, for example, refused to let Americans navigate the Mississippi and ship their products and goods to sea unless they paid export fees in New Orleans. British troops, meanwhile, remained in North America, refusing to leave the western frontier until Americans honored the peace treaty and paid their debts to England. Some state governments, however, complicated matters by passing laws to create obstacles to collecting these debts.

Meanwhile, American settlers who felt threatened by Native Americans in the Ohio River Valley demanded military protection. Raising funds to strengthen the army was hard to do, given that the congress had not yet paid

Daniel Shays led farmers in rebellion in Massachusetts.

many of the soldiers who had fought in the Revolution. In addition, the army was becoming even more undisciplined and demoralized.

Economic Hard Times

A postwar depression added to the woes of the new nation. A key problem was that America's staggering war debts had to be paid and revenues had been reduced because trade with England had been cut off during the war. Although America again traded with its former foe after the war, the new nation now imported more than it exported. This trade

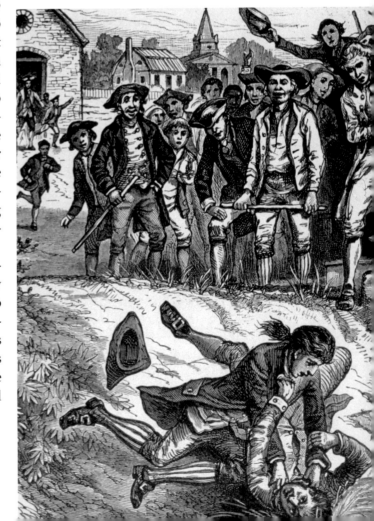

Hamilton Identifies Flaws in the Military

Alexander Hamilton, statesman and a veteran of the Revolutionary War, was a supporter of a strong national government and an early critic of the Articles of Confederation. This extract of his September 3, 1780, letter to James Duane, a New York delegate to the Confederation Congress, indicates his worry that the Articles of Confederation fail to provide a strong army, necessary for the unity and defense of a nation:

The fundamental defect is a want [lack] of power in Congress. It is hardly worth while to show in what this consists, as it seems to be universally acknowledged, or to point to how it has happened, as the only question is how to remedy it. . . . The entire formation and disposal of our military forces ought to belong to Congress. It is an essential cement of the union; and it ought to be the policy of Congress to destroy all ideas of state attachment in the army and make it look up wholly to them. . . . Already some of the lines of the army would obey their states in opposition to Congress. . . . Without a speedy change the army must dissolve; it is now a mob, rather than an army, without clothing, without pay, without provision, without morals, without discipline.

Quoted in Richard Haesly, ed., *The Constitutional Convention.* San Diego: Greenhaven, 2002, pp. 44–47.

imbalance resulted in vast amounts of silver and gold being sent from America to England. Making matters worse, some states continued issuing paper money to pay off their debts even though there was no gold in their treasuries to back the currency.

Farmers were hit especially hard. Their failure to make debt payments or pay taxes resulted in foreclosures that forced them off their farms. Some even ended up in debtors' prisons. Pure desperation drove many farmers to demand that their state legislatures enact laws that delayed or eased their debt payments. Lawmakers, however, routinely rebuffed these requests.

In Massachusetts many farmers were incensed that the merchants who seized farmlands for debt failures were often members of the state legislature that denied their requests for help. Adding insult to injury, farmers lost the right to vote when their property was taken.

Tensions finally exploded when Daniel Shays, a farmer and Revolutionary War hero, led twelve hundred angry farmers in armed rebellion in Massachusetts. Shays's men halted auctions of bankrupted farms, disrupted court proceedings, and in some cases robbed wealthy businessmen. They also had plans to take control of a store of muskets at a Springfield arsenal.

Although state troops easily suppressed the uprising, Shays's Rebellion sent shock waves throughout the thirteen states and caused many to wonder if another revolution was brewing. Washington wrote, "I predict the worst consequences for a half-starved, limping government, always moving upon crutches and tottering at every step.... I do not conceive we can exist long as a nation without having lodged somewhere a power which will pervade the whole Union."[28]

Seeking a Remedy

Across the nation, many powerful leaders agreed that something must be done to strengthen the central government if America was to survive as a republic. New York's Alexander Hamilton, a brilliant politician who had once served as Washington's aide-de-camp and an outspoken advocate of a strong national government, complained, "The confederation itself is defective and requires to be altered; it is neither fit for war, nor peace."[29]

James Madison, a congressman from Virginia, also recognized the need for correcting weaknesses in the national government. He brought his concerns to a meeting at Annapolis, Maryland, initially set up to discuss navigation problems Virginia and Maryland were having on the Potomac River. Here Madison asked the delegates to consider bigger issues

and proposed that they ask the congress to set up a national convention for the purpose of revising the Articles of Confederation.

A majority of congress members agreed with the idea and authorized the convention to begin at Philadelphia on May 14, 1787. Franklin wrote Jefferson, describing the importance of the upcoming convention, "Our federal constitution is generally thought defective, and

James Madison wanted a national convention to be created in order to revise the Articles of Confederation.

a convention, first proposed by Virginia, and since recommended by Congress, is to assemble here next month, to revise it and propose amendments. . . . If it does not do good it will do harm, as it will show that we have not the wisdom enough among us to govern ourselves."[30]

Though many Americans agreed that such a convention was necessary, they were at odds over what kinds of revisions they should make. Some wanted a large, powerful government to provide national security. Others, however, worried that such a government would threaten their liberties; instead they favored keeping state governments strong and independent. The delegates traveling to Philadelphia soon found out that the way to address these opposite views rested on a very delicate balance.

Chapter Five

Hammering Out a Constitution

Congress urged the state legislatures to send as many delegates as they could to the upcoming convention. Out of the seventy-four men selected, however, only fifty-five eventually took part. Often traveling with wives and children, the delegates came from every state except Rhode Island, which refused to participate. Not everyone, however, arrived by opening day. Unexpected delays and having to travel on dirt roads by horse-drawn coach meant some journeys often took weeks.

Once the delegates reached Philadelphia, they stayed in hotels, lodges, and private dwellings. Many preferred the city's elegant Indian Queen hotel as their home for the next four months. Historian Charles Mee provides this description of their accommodations:

The guests sat at . . . large round tables, smoking long-stemmed clay pipes and drinking toddies, flips, lemonade laced with wine, bowls of punch, or Madeira, reading British or American papers and magazines, checking the notices and broadsides tacked up near the bar, exchanging news and gossips in what was still, as it had been for scores of years, the quintessentially [typically] natural setting for politics in America."[31]

Among the talented individuals who arrived in Philadelphia were some of America's greatest leaders—men whom Jefferson described as "demi-gods." Hamilton came from New York. Another was Franklin, the nation's elder statesman from Pennsylvania. The Virginia legislature sent two noted political leaders: George Mason, author of the Virginia Bill of Rights, and James Madison.

Washington, however, lent the greatest prestige to the great gathering. Though a national war hero, he was reluctant to leave

George Mason was the author of the Virginia Bill of Rights.

his farm and attend the convention. Washington also suffered from rheumatism and had told the organizers of another meeting of retired officers also being held in Philadelphia that he could not attend their affair. Madison, however, persuaded Washington that his presence at the convention would be a great service to his country.

The general soon joined a distinguished group of delegates. Forty-two of them had participated in the Continental Congress. Several had created and served in state governments. Thirty fought in the American Revolution and eight signed the Declaration of Independence. Though the delegates did not represent the full spectrum of American society, they reflected an array of professions and occupations. As merchants, farmers, plantation owners, and financiers, they brought to the convention a wealth of political thought, tradition, and experience. Like most other Americans, they also cherished the heritage of rights that evolved in England. Many delegates were also avid readers of history and knew the strengths and weaknesses of ancient republics such as Carthage and Rome; they used this historical perspective to guide them in addressing the nation's problems of governance. All delegates also understood that they themselves were making history in Philadelphia.

Self-interest, of course, also informed the opinions of the delegates. In addition, Christianity and deism (a belief system based on the concept that the universe works according to precise natural laws and was created by an indifferent supernatural being that was not swayed by prayer or rituals) played large roles in the lives of the men who gathered at Philadelphia. However, it was the ongoing Enlightenment with its emphasis on reason, skepticism, and clarity of thought that made the biggest impact on how most delegates thought about the nature of government.

The delegates, like their fellow Americans, differed greatly over what form of government they thought was best for their nation. However, most agreed that the Articles of Confederation had failed. There was also consensus that the congress needed more authority to regulate commerce and levy taxes to support a military that would protect their new nation.

Constitutional Character Sketches

Thanks to the written observations of William Pierce, a Georgia delegate at the Constitutional Convention, modern readers have vivid character sketches of some of the major participants in the debates that forged the U.S. Constitution. The following is Pierce's description of Alexander Hamilton of New York:

Col. [Alexander] Hamilton is deservedly celebrated for his talents. He is a practitioner of the law, and reputed to be a finished scholar . . . it is my opinion that he is rather a convincing Speaker, than a blazing orator. Col. Hamilton requires time to think—he enquires into every part of his subject with the searchings of philosophy, and when he comes forward he comes highly charged with interesting matter; there is no skimming over the surface of a subject with him; he must sink to the bottom to see what foundation it rests on. His language is not always equal, sometimes didactic, . . . at others light and tripping . . . he rambles just enough to strike and keep up the attention. He is about 33 years old, of small stature, and lean. His manners are tinctured [tinted] with stiffness, and sometimes with a degree of vanity that is highly disagreeable.

Quoted in Richard Haesly, ed., *The Constitutional Convention*. San Diego: Greenhaven, 2002, pp. 80–81.

The Absence of Top Leaders

Several of America's top leaders did not attend the convention. Jefferson and John Adams were serving as ambassadors in Europe, and John Jay, a respected statesman and a future chief justice of the U.S. Supreme Court, was in New York serving as the secretary for foreign affairs. Thomas Paine, the firebrand pamphleteer of the Revolution, was also in Europe on business.

Skepticism, however, kept away the fiery orator Patrick Henry. Though Henry was selected to represent Virginia, he refused the position. "I smelt a rat,"[32] he said, revealing his suspicion that the convention intended to overthrow the power of the states.

Another radical, Sam Adams, former leader of the Sons of Liberty, did not appear because he was rejected as a delegate by the Massachusetts legislature, which thought his fiery nature was inappropriate for the convention where consensus and compromise, not confrontation and dramatic oratory, were needed.

Others too thought that a calm, thoughtful approach was the best way to restructure America's government. One of them was Madison, who arrived three weeks before the opening date. Months earlier, upon request, Jefferson had sent Madison hundreds of books on government, law, and philosophy to help the intellectual prepare his thoughts for the convention. For years Madison had believed the "league of friendship" between the thirteen states had failed, and

Patrick Henry declined to attend the Constitutional Convention.

now, as he studied by candlelight in the early morning hours waiting for the others to arrive, he became convinced it was time for a new constitution.

The Delegates Arrive

By May 25 enough delegates had arrived to get the convention underway at the Philadelphia statehouse. One of the first items of business was to elect Washington to preside over the convention. George Wythe of Virginia presented the rules: Among other restrictions, delegates could not whisper, pass notes, or read books or newspapers when another was speaking. Each state was allowed to cast one vote regardless of how many delegates were present.

The delegates also adopted a parliamentary procedure called the "committee of the whole." Under this informal system, members could debate issues as they would in one large committee rather than a legislative body; they could also vote but not be bound by their votes if they changed their minds as arguments unfolded. This was done to encourage thinking and discussion.

Several delegates kept sketch notes during the proceedings, but Madison made the best and most complete notes that are still read today. He never missed a meeting.

Edmund Randolph, the thirty-four-year-old Virginia governor, opened the convention to main business when he rose and proposed a new constitution that he and Madison had discussed at the

George Washington was chosen to preside over the convention.

Indian Queen tavern. Their Virginia Plan called for a strong federal, or national, government made up three branches—executive, judicial, and legislative. Each of these branches would be able to check, or balance, the power of the others. The national government could also veto state laws.

At first Madison's suggestion for a three-part government did not generate much controversy. Most delegates were familiar with the idea, because it was already the basis for many state governments. Besides, they understood that his proposal was meant as a springboard for discussion.

Another delegate, Charles Pinckney, a twenty-nine-year-old South Carolina planter, offered another proposal. Because surviving documents are not clear on what Pinckney presented that opening day, historians are not sure what his plan entailed. Most, however, believe that though it contained some of the same principles introduced by Randolph, it was more of a call for revisions to the Articles of Confederation than for a comprehensive new constitution. Whatever Pinckney's plan was, the convention ignored it. Thus, by the end of the day Madison and Randolph had managed to make their constitution the central issue of debate.

Debating the Virginia Plan

The next day the delegates moved their proceedings to the second floor of the Convention Hall and agreed to keep their talks secret and not to discuss them outside the statehouse. Sentries were posted outside the door to keep out unauthorized people.

Ten days of debate followed as delegates discussed many important questions posed by the Virginia Plan. What was meant by the phrase, the *federal government*? Did *federal* mean supreme? Or did it imply a compact among the states? Did the Virginia Plan intend to overthrow state government? At one point, Gouverneur Morris, a tall, sarcastic, peg-legged, courtly looking man from Pennsylvania, defended the call for a strong national government, saying it was necessary to ward off a worse form of government. "We had better take a supreme government now than a despot [dictator] twenty years hence—for come he must,"[33] he said.

Delegates also quarreled over details for a bicameral, or two-house, legislature. Under the Virginia Plan the number of representatives for each house would be based on population, thus giving the advantage to more populated states. However, any fears the smaller states had of being overshadowed by more populous states were misguided, Randolph explained. After all, he added, a small state may very well have more in common with a neighboring large state than it would with a different small and distant state.

Another question emerged: Should representation be based on how much a state pays in taxes or on population? At this point, a dangerous side issue came into play: slavery.

At the time slavery prospered in the South and had almost vanished in the North. Many northern delegates considered

Setting Up the Debate Rules

The following excerpt of the rules for discussion used by the delegates at the Constitutional Convention comes from The Debates in the Several State Conventions on the Adoption of the Federal Constitution, *a five-volume collection compiled by Jonathan Elliot in the mid-nineteenth century.*

Every member, rising to speak, shall address the president; and, whilst he shall be speaking, none shall pass between them, or hold discourse with another, or read a book, pamphlet, or paper, printed or manuscript.

And of two members rising at the same time, the president shall name him who shall be first heard.

A member shall not speak oftener than twice, without special leave, upon the same question; and not the second time, before every other, who had been silent, shall have been heard, if he choose to speak upon the subject.

A motion made and seconded shall be repeated, and if written, as it shall be when any member shall so require, read aloud, by the secretary, before it shall be debated; and may be withdrawn at any time before the vote upon it shall have been declared. . . .

A member may be called to order by any other member, as well as by the president, and may be allowed to explain his conduct, or expressions, supposed to be reprehensible [in the wrong]; and all questions of order shall be decided by the president, without appeal or debate. . . .

When the house shall adjourn, every member shall stand in his place until the president pass him.

Jonathan Elliot, *The Debates in the Several State Conventions on the Adoption of the Federal Constitution.* Philadelphia: J. B. Lippincott, 1896.

Delegates at the convention debated over many components of the Virginia Plan.

Franklin Reassures the Delegates

Like many of the delegates at the Constitutional Convention, Benjamin Franklin had doubts about certain parts of the new Constitution. However, when the convention's work was done, he wrote a speech that praised his fellow delegates for their accomplishments and their willingness to compromise. After hearing Franklin's words, excerpted here, many delegates overcame their reservations about the Constitution and signed it.

I agree to this Constitution with all its faults—if they are such—because I think a general government necessary for us . . . I doubt, too whether any other convention we can obtain may be able to make a better Constitution; for, when you assemble a number of men, to have the advantage of their joint wisdom, you inevitably assemble with those men all their prejudices, their passions, their errors of opinion, their local interests, and their selfish views. From such an assembly can a perfect production be expected?

It therefore astonishes me . . . to find this system approaching as near to perfection as it does; and I think it will astonish our enemies, who are waiting with confidence to hear that our councils are confounded . . . and that our States are on the point of separation, only to meet hereafter for the purpose of cutting one another's throats. Thus I consent, sire, to this Constitution because I expect no better, and because I am not sure that it is not the best.

Quoted in Walter Isaacson, *Benjamin Franklin: An American Life.* New York: Simon & Schuster, 2003, pp. 457–58.

the enslavement of blacks as immoral and something to be eradicated by law. Southerners, on the other hand, claimed that slaves were property, and protection of property was a fundamental duty of government. Until now, delegates had largely ignored this issue, fearing it would disrupt, if not ruin, the convention.

But by June, slavery was a hot topic. In addition to arguing the moral aspects of slavery, some delegates also wondered how slaves would be considered in terms of taxes. Pierce Butler of South Carolina suggested that states that paid more in property taxes should have more power in Congress. To this, Massachusetts's Elbridge Gerry demanded to know how slaves should be counted. "Blacks are property," he said, "and are used to the south-ward as horses and cattle to the north-ward. Why then, should not horses and cattle have the right of representation in the North?"[34]

Gerry's sarcastic question underscored a larger issue: How should slaves be counted for purposes of representation? Slave state delegates wanted slaves included in their population counts to boost their number of representatives, although they had no intention of letting slaves vote. Northern delegates, meanwhile, had no intention of letting southern states gain political power by means of what many considered an evil institution. The convention would not solve this problem until August.

Other matters, meanwhile, also sparked controversy. Among them was the question of whether the country needed a president—one that ran a separate branch of government and did not preside over the legislature. Some asserted that an individual with great powers was needed to protect the nation in a crisis. Others thought the country needed several executives. Critics, however,

feared that such power, whether concentrated in the hands of one person or many, inevitably set the stage for dictatorship and tyranny. Some wanted to know how long a president's term of office should be.

Enduring Flies and Heat

As the debate wore on, delegates sweltered in the summer heat, made worse because all windows of the state house were closed to keep out the swarms of black flies that infested Philadelphia. The flies tormented the delegates, buzzing and stinging them and landing on their faces all day long. As the French minister of foreign affairs Charles Talleyrand once observed of Philadelphia's fly epidemic, "If one writes, the paper is spotted with fly-speck. If a woman is dressed in white, her dress is in like manner spoiled."[35]

Enduring the heat and the flies, the delegates continued their deliberations. By now they agreed that three branches of government with provisions for a system of "checks and balances" were necessary to curb power. But they still could not reach consensus on the issue of proportionate representation versus equal representation.

Rival Plans Emerge

By June 15 the convention took a new turn. William Patterson of New Jersey, frustrated with the Virginia Plan, presented his own to the convention. His plan called for a one-house legislature

William Patterson presented his own plan at the convention, but it was rejected.

that allowed each state, big or small, one vote. As he spoke, delegates realized that the intent of this New Jersey Plan was for the nation to remain as a gathering of states with equal power and not as an assembly of individual Americans. Patterson's plan, in effect, kept basic principles of the Articles of Confederation intact, except that Congress would have the power to tax and regulate business.

The convention debated Patterson's proposal for three days and then rejected it. On June 18 Hamilton spent six hours offering yet another proposal, though it received no support. Among other things, critics disliked his call for an executive that would serve for life and have the power to veto all laws. To many this sounded like a monarchy. Hamilton left the convention not long afterward.

Though the rival plans had been voted down, the representatives of the smaller states had clarified their unhappiness with the Virginia Plan. Some were so angry that they threatened to leave the convention unless provisions were made for at least one house based on population. Delaware's Gunford Bedford warned that if the larger states imposed a strong national government, "The small ones will find some foreign ally of more honor and good faith, who will take them by the hand and do them justice."[36]

Bedford's rash remarks sent shock waves throughout the convention. Other delegates quickly rebuked him. Rufus King from Massachusetts declared, "For myself whatever may be my distress I will never court a foreign power to assist in relieving myself from it."[37]

A Compromise to Calm the Convention

Bitter debate—especially over the representation question—raged until the end of June. By now the debate had become so bitter and hostile that Franklin, a man commonly noted for his religious skepticism, suggested that a clergyman should open each session with a prayer to lessen the hostility. Upon hearing this, Hamilton is reported to have snapped that the convention could do its job without "the necessity of calling in foreign aid."[38]

At last a stalemate was averted, when one of the committee members, Roger Sherman of Connecticut, rose to propose the creation of two houses of lawmakers. The number of representatives for a lower house—the House of Representatives—would be based on population. In the upper house, or the Senate, each state would have equal representation, regardless of the size of its population. Despite the good intention of the committee, Sherman's proposal drew fire from some who feared that it leaned too far in the direction of states' rights. Also, there still remained the unresolved issue of counting slaves.

A vote was finally called and resulted in a tie. Another committee, comprised of one member from each state, convened to break the impasse. At last the group recommended a compromise: A lower house would be based on population, with slaves counted as three-fifths of a person for purposes of taxes and representation only; states in an upper house would all have exactly the same number

tion, while the growing South with its slave-based economy would enjoy greater political strength in the House.

According to the compromise, voters would elect members of the House, who had to be at least twenty-six years old and serve two-year terms. State legislatures, however, would choose the country's senators, who had to be thirty years old and would serve six years at a time.

Adding the Final Details

At this point there was little left for anyone to say. It was time to put the ideas into writing. On July 24 the convention chose five men to act as a "committee of detail" to draft a constitution based on the agreements reached during debate. On August 6 the convention met again. As delegates read their draft copies, controversy flared up again. Suddenly, southern delegates complained that if Congress, dominated by northern states, had the power to regulate commerce, it could, through export taxes, hurt the South's economy.

The slavery issue stirred once more, putting the convention in an uproar. Even Morris, a defender of wealth, joined other critics from the North and denounced slavery as

Roger Sherman proposed the creation of the House of Representatives and the Senate.

of representatives. Such a system benefited almost all the states. In the Senate, northern states would enjoy greater representation in relation to their popula-

Thomas Paine Expresses His Views on God

Like many of the creators of the U.S. Constitution, Thomas Paine held deist beliefs. Here is a sampling of his thoughts that appear in his book Age of Reason:

I believe in one God, and no more; and I hope for happiness beyond this life.

I believe in the equality of man; and I believe that religious duties consist in doing justice, loving mercy, and endeavouring to make our fellow creatures happy. . . .

I do not believe in the creed professed by the Jewish church, by the Roman church, by the Greek church, by the Turkish church, by the Protestant church, nor by any church that I know of. My own mind is my own church.

All national institutions of churches, whether Jewish, Christian, or Turkish, appear to me no other than human inventions, set up to terrify and enslave mankind, and monopolize power and profit. . . .

Every national church or religion has established itself by pretending some special mission from God, communicated to certain individuals. The Jews have their Moses; the Christians their Jesus Christ, their apostles, and saints; and the Turks their Mahomet, as if the way to God was not open to every man alike.

Each of those churches show certain books, which they call revelation, or the word of God. . . . Each of those churches accuse the other of unbelief; and, for my own part, I disbelieve them all.

Quoted in W.W. Norton, *The Age of Reason:* "Thomas Paine on Deism," *World Civilizations.* www.wwnorton. com/college/history/ralph/workbook/ralprs24b.htm.

"the curse of heaven on the states where it prevailed."[39]

Incensed southerners retorted that slavery was essential to their economy and way of life. The anger among the southern faction was so strong that John Rutledge of South Carolina warned that the only question left was "whether the Southern states shall or shall not be parties to the Union."[40]

Finally, the convention produced another compromise. The antislavery faction agreed to a provision in the constitution that denied Congress the authority to regulate the slave trade before 1808. Any slaves imported during this time, however, would be subject to an import tax. Northerners also agreed that slave owners could recover slaves who escaped to other states. In return, southerners accepted constitutional language that made it easier for northern states to get certain navigation advantages they had long desired. Before the Revolution, England had required that the colonists export their goods on British ships. Southerners, who had few merchant ships, had long worried that new laws could be passed that would require goods to be shipped on American vessels. Because the North owned most of the new nation's seagoing vessels, southerners feared that northern states could control the South's economy if lawmakers passed such a requirement; thus, southern delegates wanted the constitution to require a two-thirds majority to make difficult the passage of any navigation acts. Now, though, because southerners received concessions on the slave issue, they agreed that the two-thirds requirement be dropped.

The compromise also set forth provisions for the new government to coin money, regulate commerce, and make laws. A federal system was also set up that divided power among a lawmaking body, a presidency that executes or carries out the laws, and a court system that enforces them. To assure that no branch would become too powerful, a system of checks and balances was also created. For example, a president may veto, or cancel, a law passed by Congress. The lawmakers, however, can override his objection with a two-thirds majority.

One sticking point remained: Many delegates complained that the plan they were developing had no bill of rights—one that stated explicitly the rights of citizens. Though this omission troubled many delegates, the consensus was that such a bill was not needed at this point. Most state constitutions, some argued, already had such a bill. Moreover, others added, adding a bill of rights might be akin to waving a red flag to the citizenry that there was something suspicious about the new document.

Delegates worked out another compromise on electing a president. They crafted language that allowed only one executive—a person at least thirty-five years old and born in the United States—to serve for four years and be eligible to run for reelection. However, instead of voting directly for a president, voters would elect presidential electors to cast their votes for the best candidate.

In a bow to the advocates of states' rights, delegates agreed that Congress would not be able to declare state laws unconstitutional. In time, however, the federal judiciary would assume this responsibility.

Deciding How to Ratify

The delegates faced yet another big question: Who should approve, or ratify, the constitution? One idea contained in the Virginia Plan was that after the congress had given its approval to the process, an assembly composed of representatives from the states, elected by the people, should convene and vote.

This idea was not popular, nor was calling for another national convention. Delegates also disliked letting the various state legislatures debate and vote on the constitution. Many suspected that smaller states would be hostile to the constitution and sabotage ratification efforts.

Finally, the delegates decided the constitution was so important that it demanded popular ratification. This meant that once the congress ratified the document, states would set up special conventions where delegates would debate and vote on ratification. The convention

The signing of the U.S. Constitution.

further decided that ratification required approval of nine of the thirteen states, not a unanimous vote.

Final Editing

With delegates on the verge of collapse, another special working group—the committee of style and arrangement—put the final touches on the constitution. At last, the final document was ready on September 12. Among the most impor-tant alterations was the changing of the words in the preamble from "We, the people of the States of North Carolina, Virginia, Massachusetts, [and so forth]" to "We, the people of the United States." The new phrase was more than a change in style; it also indicated that the consti-tution was a framework for a govern-ment that bound together the American people, not states, as the Articles of Con-federation had done.

Before the delegates could go home, Franklin asked them to join him in signing the historic document. He, like most, if not all, the delegates, had reservations about their work. Franklin, however, was amazed that they had done so well. A perfect document, he told his colleagues, would never be possible, given the diversity of opinion in the convention. "Thus," he said, "I consent, Sir, to this Constitution because I expect no better and because I am not sure that it is not the best."[41]

Morris also had objections, but signed anyway. "The moment this plan goes forth," he predicted, "all other considerations will be laid aside and the great question will be, shall there be a national government or not? This must take place, or a general anarchy will be the alternative."[42]

Three delegates had such strong misgivings over the constitution, however, that they could not sign. Randolph, who had introduced the Virginia Plan, now said, "In refusing to sign the Constitution, I take a step which may be the most awful of my life, but it is not possible for me to hesitate, much less change."[43] Gerry and Mason also refused to sign.

All others, except those who had left the convention, affixed their signatures to the document they had struggled to forge. After the signing, the convention adjourned. Delegates dined at a local tavern, made their farewells, and prepared for their long journeys home. Their work was done.

Chapter Six

Ratifying the Constitution

O nce the convention ended, copies of the Constitution were printed at a nearby shop and sent to the Continental Congress for approval. Now a long waiting period began as delegates ventured home, anticipating what the American people would say about the work done at Philadelphia on their behalf.

Ten of the departing delegates, who were also members of the congress, used their positions to shepherd the constitution through a September session in New York. Although the congress did not endorse the constitution, it transmitted the document to the thirteen states on September 28.

As the states prepared their ratification conferences, the American public learned the details of the proposed constitution from pamphlets and newspapers. Ratification became an issue for the whole nation, as Americans from all walks of life took part in vigorous discussions in taverns, homes, churches, and other public places.

It soon became clear that the nation was sharply divided over ratification. As a national debate unfolded, most Americans generally fell into two camps: the federalists, who favored ratification, or their opponents, the anti-federalists.

Anti-federalist "Centinel" essays opposing ratification appeared around the country. Still more attacks arrived in published articles under the name pen name "Cato." The federalists fought back: Hamilton, Jay, and Madison published eighty-five brilliant essays known as the *Federalist Papers*. These writings dissected the flaws of the Articles of Confederation and expounded on the need for a robust federal government. Today, the *Federalist Papers* remains as one of the best guides to the formative ideas of the Constitution.

A National Debate

Federalists enjoyed a few advantages in the debate. For one thing, the Constitution represented the work of a group of respected national leaders, such as Washington and Franklin. Federalists also offered many Americans something to rally behind—a specific plan to save the union from dissolution.

In contrast, as Madison noted of the Massachusetts anti-federalists, "There was not a single character capable of uniting their wills or directing their measures.... They had no plan whatever."[44] Instead, writes historian Catherine Drinker Bowen, "Anti-federalists worked on the people's

Title page of The Federalist Papers.

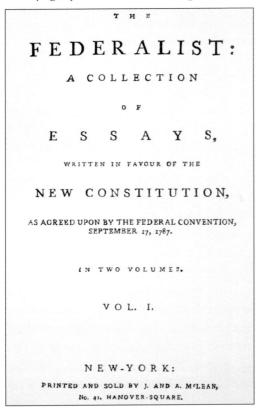

THE

FEDERALIST:

A COLLECTION

OF

ESSAYS,

WRITTEN IN FAVOUR OF THE

NEW CONSTITUTION,

AS AGREED UPON BY THE FEDERAL CONVENTION,
SEPTEMBER 17, 1787.

IN TWO VOLUMES.

VOL. I.

NEW-YORK:

PRINTED AND SOLD BY J. AND A. McLEAN,
No. 41, HANOVER-SQUARE.

fear; they viewed with alarm, harped on the novelty, the experimental nature of the program."[45] Some of these critics charged that delegates had created the Constitution in secrecy and produced a document that was intended to benefit the wealthy and the privileged. A Massachusetts anti-federalist complained, "These lawyers, and men of learning and moneyed men, that ...make us poor illiterate people swallow down the pill ... they will swallow up all us little folks ... just as the whale swallowed up Jonah!"[46]

Critics also warned that a strong federal government would take away their liberties. Some suggested that if a capital city, such as Washington, D.C., was established as called for in the Constitution, Americans could expect it to become a dangerous armed camp. Setting up a vice presidency was also treacherous because it could create a rival to the president. Various church leaders complained that framers did not make Christianity part of the Constitution. One Protestant Christian, however, "shuddered at the idea that Roman Catholics, papists and pagans might be introduced into office and that popery [the Catholic leadership] and the Inquisition [torture once used by the Church] may be established in America."[47]

Anti-federalists successfully created a strong resistance to the Constitution, but their cause was weakened because they were divided in their opposition. Northern critics, for example, complained that the Constitution did not end slavery, while southern planters argued it did not fully protect the institution.

Explaining the Need for a Constitution

The following paragraphs are part of a letter written by a special committee and approved by the convention that explains why the convention decided to draft a plan for a new government instead of revising the old one:

It is obviously impracticable in the federal government of these states to secure all rights of independent sovereignty [independent power] to each, and yet provide for the interest and safety of all. Individuals entering into society must give up a share of liberty to preserve the rest. The magnitude of the sacrifice must depend as well on situation and circumstance as on the object to be obtained. It is at all times difficult to draw . . . the line between those rights which must be surrendered and those which may be reserved; and on the present occasion, this difficulty was increased by a difference among the several states as to their situation, extent, habits and particular interests.

In all our deliberations on this subject we kept steadily in our view that which appears to us the greatest interest of every true American: the consolidation of our union . . . thus the Constitution which we now present is the result of a spirit of . . . [friendship and compromise].

That it will meet the full and entire approbation [approval] of every state is not perhaps to be expected; but . . . that it may promote the lasting welfare of the country so dear to us all, and secure her freedom and happiness, is our most ardent [passionate] wish.

Quoted in William Peters, *A More Perfect Union: The Making of the United States Constitution*. New York: Crown, 1987, p. 216.

Economic and social factors often determined which side of the argument Americans chose. Many bankers, factory owners, professionals, wealthy landowners, and Revolutionary War officers filled the ranks of federalists. Anti-federalists, meanwhile, tended to be tradesmen, farmers, and those who supported economic policies that favored debtors. In addition, some state government officials also opposed ratification because they feared losing power and control to a central government. As historian Richard B. Morris explains: "The anti federalists often looked very much like a group of state and local officeholders concerned about their vested interests."[48]

The anti-ratification movement had roots in the revolutionary period. Memories of British oppression were still fresh for many, and they feared a strong national government would cause similar problems. Older Americans, in fact, who remembered the abuses of the oppressive British government, were more likely than younger people to oppose a new central government. Ironically, many of the revolutionary-era Americans, once deemed as radicals, now looked at a younger generation of Constitution supporters as the new radicals.

Geography also played a role in dividing America into two camps. According to author William Peters,

> Federalist power was located mostly in the settled, eastern sections of the states. Anti-federalism was generally strongest in the backcountry and frontier areas, regions that had been underrepresented in the Convention. Far from the centers of political power in their own states, backcountry Americans saw themselves as certain to be even more remote from the seat of some new national government.[49]

Ratification Conventions Get Underway

The debate in the American public mirrored the clashes taking place in the state ratification conventions. On September 28, 1787, Pennsylvania's federalists were so eager to ratify that they tried to push a proposal through the state assembly authorizing a ratification convention, even though official notification from the congress concerning the Constitution had not yet arrived. When nineteen anti-federalists boycotted the session to prevent having the required minimum number of lawmakers, an angry mob forcibly abducted two of them from a nearby boardinghouse and dragged them kicking and fighting into the statehouse. The assembly now had a quorum, which established the first Tuesday in November as the day to vote for convention delegates.

At last, the Pennsylvania ratification convention got underway on November 21, 1787. Though outnumbered, anti-federalists rose in the statehouse to fight ratification. Some complained that the constitutional convention exceeded its

James Wilson was attacked by anti-federalists during Pennsylvania's debate on ratifying the U.S. Constitution.

authority. Others were upset that the Constitution had no bill of rights.

Any hopes among federalists that Pennsylvania would be the first to ratify were dashed when news came that Delaware had unanimously approved the Constitution on December 7 after just five days of debate. Like other small states, Delaware now saw its role reversed from what it was during the constitutional convention. Under the final draft of the Constitution, smaller states like Delaware stood to gain power and influence that exceeded their population or wealth.

Debate in Pennsylvania raged on for weeks. Tempers ran high even after delegates finally ratified the Constitution on December 12. Violence later erupted when a group of angry anti-federalists physically attacked James Wilson, a proponent of the Constitution, when he tried to make a celebratory speech. An old soldier threw himself across Wilson and kept him from being killed.

By January 9, 1788, Georgia, Connecticut, and New Jersey had also voted for ratification. A month of contentious debate in Boston, Massachusetts, ended in favor of the federalists when distinguished anti-federalists Sam Adams and Hancock changed their minds and joined the federalists. The state assembly ratified the Constitution with recommenda-

Ratification of the U.S. Constitution

RATIFICATION OF THE U.S. CONSTITUTION

State	Date Ratified	Vote
Delaware	December 7, 1787	30 for, 0 against
Pennsylvania	December 12, 1787	46 for, 23 against
New Jersey	December 18, 1787	38 for, 0 against
Connecticut	January 9, 1788	128 for, 40 against
Georgia	February 2, 1788	26 for, 0 against
Massachusetts	February 6, 1788	187 for, 168 against
Maryland	April 28, 1788	63 for, 11 against
South Carolina	May 23, 1788	149 for, 73 against
New Hampshire	June 21, 1788	57 for, 47 against
Virginia	June 25, 1788	89 for, 79 against
New York	July 26, 1788	30 for, 27 against
North Carolina	November 21, 1789	194 for, 77 against
Rhode Island	May 29, 1790	34 for, 32 against

Source: "Ratification Dates and Votes," *The U.S. Constitution Online,* http://www.usconstitution.net/ratifications.html.

tions that it be amended in the future. During the spring, Maryland also voted for ratification after just five days of discussion, by a vote of sixty-three to eleven. Twelve anti-federalists, however, signed a letter of protest: "We consider the proposed form of government very defective, and that the liberty and happiness of the people will be endangered if the system be not greatly changed and altered."[50] Almost a month later South Carolina also ratified the Constitution.

Though the slavery issued bitterly divided delegates in New Hampshire, they eventually voted to ratify on June 21, with a vote of fifty-seven to forty-seven, becoming the necessary ninth state to make the Constitution legal. A new union had officially formed.

Pressure Mounts on Big States

Two of the nation's most important states, though, had not yet voted. Virginia was essential to the nation because of its size, and New York because of its important location on the Atlantic. Many Americans could not conceive of how the nation could function without them. For the moment however, these states were still locked in controversy.

In Virginia, where anti-federalists were in the majority, Colonel William Grayson mocked the federalist claim that a federal government was needed to ward off national threats:

Pennsylvania and Maryland are to fall upon us from the north like the Goths and Vandals of old . . . the In-

dians are to invade us from our rears . . . And the Carolinians from the South, mounted on alligators, I presume, are to come and destroy our cornfields and eat up our little children. These Sir, are the mighty dangers which await us if we reject the Constitution.[51]

Patrick Henry warned, "The American spirit, assisted by the ropes and chains of consolidation [federalism] is about to convert this country into a powerful and mighty empire. . . . There be no checks, no real balances in this government."[52]

Despite such colorful rhetoric, anti-federalists were losing the battle in Virginia. On the first day of debate, Edmund Randolph shocked and angered his anti-federalist allies by defecting to the other side. He explained that he had taken this action to preserve the nation. The union "is the anchor of our political salvation; and I will assent to the lopping off this limb," he said, pointing to his arm, "before I assent to the dissolution of the union."[53]

A spate of angry attacks on Randolph and federalism could not stop a majority of the delegation from ratifying on June 25. Delegates also called for amendments when the First Congress convened.

Many anti-federalists in Virginia, however, found defeat hard to take. At a protest meeting in Richmond they discussed ways to prevent the Constitution from working. Patrick Henry, however, counseled them to drop the matter. Then

A Ratification Song

Like many other places in America, Boston erupted into celebration after its state convention ratified the Constitution. In addition to the cheers, toasts, and ringing of church bells, Bostonians sang this song to the tune of "Yankee Doodle":

The 'Vention did in Boston meet,

The State House could not hold 'em,

So then they went to Fed'ral Steet,

And there the truth was told 'em. . . .

And ev'ry morning went to prayer,

And then began disputing,

Till oppositions silenced were,

By arguments refuting.

Then 'Squire Hancock like a man,

Who dearly loved the nation,

By a conciliatory plan,

Prevented much vexation.

He made a woundy Fed'ral speech,

With sense and elocution;

And then the 'Vention did beseech

T' adopt the Constitution.

Now politicians of all kinds,

Who are not yet decided,

May see how Yankees speak their minds,

And yet are not divided.

So here I end my Fed'ral song,

Composed of thirteen verses;

May agriculture flourish long

And commerce fill our purses!

Quoted in Catherine Drinker Bowen, *Miracle at Philadelphia: The Story of the Constitutional Convention, May to September 1787.* Boston: Little, Brown, 1966, pp. 291–92.

he urged his fellow anti-federalists "as true and faithful republicans [members of a republic] you had all better go home."[54]

News that Virginia had ratified the Constitution rattled the anti-federalists in New York, but they refused to capitulate. One anti-federalist proposed that New York should be able to quit the new union if its amendment suggestions were not adopted. In response, Hamilton suggested that New York City and the southern counties should join the union without upstate New York. Neither motion, however, won approval. On July 26 New York also voted for ratification. Delegates recommended a bill of rights and thirty-two other amendments.

As other states celebrated ratification with parades and marches, North Carolina and Rhode Island remained undecided. North Carolina did not immediately follow Virginia's example, as many had expected. Instead, its ratification convention voted to do nothing until another national convention was held to discuss amending the Constitution.

The other states, however, showed little interest in another convention. Instead, writes Peters, "In place of a new convention, North Carolinians were soon confronted by a new government, leaving them in the uncomfortable status of foreigners."[55] The other nine states, in fact, moved forward without North Carolina and Rhode Island. On February 4, 1789, electors chose Washington as the nation's first president and John Adams as vice president. A new national government began to function, one based on the principles of the U.S. Constitution.

Adding a Bill of Rights

And when the first U.S. Congress met in March 1789 in New York City, it took up the matter of amendments. Madison, now a member of the Virginia delegation to the United States House of Representatives, kept a pledge he had made at the Virginia state ratification conference to create a bill of rights. Not trusting what could happen in another national convention, James Madison instead urged Congress to use the amendment process outlined in Article V of the Constitution. According to this article, Congress must approve an amendment by a two-thirds majority before the president signs it. Next, three-fourths of the state governments must ratify the proposed amendment within a prescribed deadline.

Out of the two hundred amendments proposed in Congress, only twelve survived. From this dozen, the states ratified ten by December 15, 1791. Known collectively as the Bill of Rights, they provide the well-known rights to freedom of religion, press, speech, peaceful assembly, and to petition government to address grievances. Americans also have the right to carry weapons and to be safe from "unreasonable searches and seizures" by law enforcement. Persons officially charged with a crime do not have to testify against themselves. Nor do they have to stand trial more than once, if by doing so puts them in "jeopardy" of imprisonment or loss of "life or limb."

The Bill of Rights. Ten amendments were ratified by December 15, 1791.

Those charged with a crime are also entitled to "due process of law," or legal procedural safeguards. In addition, they have a right to a speedy trial and a trial by jury. The accused must be informed of the specific charges brought against them, be able to confront all witnesses testifying against them, and have access to an attorney. Americans are also protected from excessive bail and cruel and unusual punishment.

By the time these rights became part of the Constitution, North Carolina and Rhode Island had also ratified the Constitution. At last, all the former colonies were united under a new national government—the country's second. The new document, however, would prove to be far more enduring than its predecessor.

Chapter Seven

An Enduring Document

The U.S. Constitution, as the cement that now binds together fifty states and 300 million people, is the nation's most cherished document. Some Americans even refer to it in reverential terms. "If America has a civic religion, the First Amendment is its central article of faith,"[56] observes Henry Louis Gates Jr., who chairs the Afro-American Studies Department at Harvard University.

Some admirers have even exalted the Constitution above all other human political achievements, because they believe it has afforded humanity a blueprint for government that excels above all others. "To live under the American Constitution is the greatest political privilege that was ever accorded to the human race,"[57] opined Calvin Coolidge, the nation's thirty-ninth president.

Others are more skeptical and point out that even with the addition of the Bill of Rights the Constitution was hardly perfect. Many critics observe that the opening words of the preamble to the U.S. Constitution, "We the People . . ." did not include women, Native Americans, blacks, or white men lacking property, none of whom had voting rights at the time. Stephen Breyer, a current associate justice of the U.S. Supreme Court writes, "As history has made clear, the original Constitution was insufficient. It did not include a majority of the nation within its 'democratic community.'"[58]

Breyer adds, though, that the Constitution also "sowed the democratic seed."[59] The document wrought by the fifty-five delegates in Philadelphia was only a beginning. For more than two centuries the American people have expanded constitutional protection through the amendment process. Some of these changes came about as a result of the Civil War. Within a few years after the conclusion of the war in 1865, the nation ratified the so-called "Civil War Amendments." The 13th Amendment outlawed slavery; the 14th provided citizenship and due process of the law to former slaves, and the 15th forbade the use of race as a means of denying the right to vote. Almost one hundred years later, during a massive civil rights movement, the nation approved the 24th Amendment in 1964 to outlaw the use of the poll tax—a tax a voter must pay—that was still being used in many southern states to discourage blacks from voting.

Democracy took another step forward with the 17th Amendment, ratified in 1913, which called for the direct election of U.S. senators. Previously, state legislatures chose senators. Seven years later, Americans ratified the 19th Amendment that gave American women suffrage, or the right to vote.

Suffrage was expanded to younger Americans in 1971, with ratification of the 26th Amendment that lowered the voting age from twenty-one to eighteen.

Not all efforts to expand equality through the amendment process, however, have been successful. Many Americans were disappointed when the country failed in the 1970s to ratify the 27th Amendment, the Equal Rights Amendment (ERA), whose supporters believed was necessary to protect females from unfair sex discrimination. Though polls showed overwhelming support for the measure among the American public, only thirty-five out of the necessary thirty-eight states had ratified the amendment by the 1979 deadline.

Crowds in the House of Representatives celebrate the passage of the 13th Amendment.

Judicial Review

In addition to the amendment process, the nation has also relied on judicial review to add constitutional safeguards. This is a procedure by which American courts decide whether certain laws or government practices violate the Constitution. Making this determination, however, is often difficult and even arbitrary. Sometimes the Court has ruled in contradictory ways about the constitutionality of law. In 1896 for instance, the Supreme Court upheld a Louisiana law that segregated railroad passengers. The Court was persuaded that segregation that allowed "equal" facilities for separate races was constitutional under the 14th Amendment. However, in 1954 in *Brown v. Board of Education of Topeka* (Kansas), a unanimous Supreme Court reversed itself, now saying that in the field of education such segregation violated the 14th Amendment, because separate educational facilities were inherently unequal. As former Chief Justice Charles Evans Hughes once observed, "The Constitution is what the judges say it is."[60]

Judicial interpretations are often controversial. Millions of Americans, for example, were shocked in 1857 when the U.S. Supreme Court used the Constitution to determine that Dred Scott, a run-

Judicial review often causes controversy. The Dred Scott case is an example where the Constitution was used by the Supreme Court to make a decision and Americans were shocked by the outcome.

away slave, could not sue for his freedom because he was another man's property and had "no rights which any white man was bound to respect."[61] Although the Court ruled that a black human being had no expectation of constitutional protections, it later decided that big businesses did deserve such protection. The Supreme Court's ruling in *Santa Clara County v. Southern Pacific Rail-*

road Co., 118 U.S. 394, paved the way for the idea of "corporate personhood"—that is, a business corporation is entitled to constitutional protection as if it were a person.

Controversy again erupted in 1973, when the U.S. Supreme Court, in *Roe v. Wade*, ruled that Texas antiabortion laws violated a woman's right to privacy under the Fourth Amendment, though the words "abortion" and "privacy" do not appear in the Constitution.

Over the years the Supreme Court has often had to rule on many issues—pornography, the medical use of marijuana, government spying on the Internet, alleged false advertising by the Nike shoe company—that the founding fathers never envisioned. Thus, justices often must interpret the "spirit" or "intent" of the Constitution as new issues emerge. They try to do this by studying previous cases, speeches made by lawmakers, and commentaries such as *The Federalist Papers* to find clues to what the original intent or principle may be. Often the task is difficult if not impossible. As Breyer notes, "The First Amendment's language says the Congress shall not abridge 'the freedom of speech'. But it does not define 'the freedom of speech' in any detail."[62]

The Constitution's framers themselves may not have welcomed this kind of scrutiny. Richard B. Morris argues that "Since the proceedings of the convention were secret and mostly not published until after James Madison's death some fifty years later,

Some presidents have claimed dubious constitutional authority. Most recently, President George W. Bush has faced criticism for his decision to wiretap phone calls without a warrant.

there is no possibility that the framers wished future interpreters to extract intention from their private debates."[63]

Critics, meanwhile, who think justices interpret the Constitution too freely, accuse them of being activist judges and interpreting the Constitution to comply with their personal beliefs. Others, however, worry that justices who use too much "judicial restraint" may render decisions that are unjust to citizens in an ever-changing world. The dilemma is summed up with this rhetorical question from historian Morris: "Is it [the Constitution] a charter carved in stone or a malleable document that can be interpreted in response to rapidly changing moral and social values and economic and technological demands?"[64]

A clue to what the framers may have replied to this question comes from Randolph, who as a member of the committee of detail in Philadelphia helped to write the finished draft of the Constitution. Instead of using specific words, he explained, the committee strove "to insert essential principles only," to keep the government from becoming "clogged" so that the Constitution could change with "times and events." Randolph added that the committee also tried "To use simple and precise language and general propositions."[65]

Over the years Congress has played a role in modifying the nature of the nation's greatest document. Under the general welfare clause of the preamble to the Constitution, for example, lawmakers have expanded economic and social opportunities for millions of citizens to a degree unimagined by many of the nation's founders. At other times, Congress has turned its own constitutional authority to declare war over to the president. Such was the case during the Vietnam War and the wars in Iraq. In 1798 Congress, perhaps in violation of the First Amendment, tried to protect the nation against foreign agitators with the Alien and Sedition Acts. One of these acts made it a crime to make "false, scandalous, and malicious" statements against Congress or the president.

Presidents have also pushed the boundaries of the Constitution. During the Civil War, Abraham Lincoln may have exceeded his authority by ordering the arrest of war protestors and denying them the constitutionally provided writ of habeas corpus—a written document informing arrested individuals of the crimes for which they are charged.

Some presidents have claimed dubious constitutional authority. During the Watergate crisis of the early 1970s, Richard Nixon, citing "executive privilege," caused a constitutional crisis by refusing to turn over information that Congress deemed important to an ongoing criminal investigation. In more recent times George W. Bush provoked concern when, in an effort to combat terrorism, he ordered the wiretapping of Americans' phone conversations without obtaining the necessary warrants first.

Sometimes political leaders have reacted to what they thought was a constitutional abuse and set in motion a process that led to another attack on the Constitution. For example, alarmed by

President Bush Proclaims Constitution Week

The following passage is part of a 2001 proclamation made by President George W. Bush to foster citizenship and to help assure the continuing legacy of the U.S. Constitution:

Today, our Nation celebrates not only the longest-lived written Constitution in world history, but also the enduring commitment of our forebears who upheld the Constitution's core principles through the travails of American history. They pursued a more perfect Union as abolitionists, as suffragists, or as civil rights activists, successfully seeking Constitutional amendments that have strengthened the protections provided to all Americans under law. In so doing, they rendered the moral resolve of our Nation stronger and clearer.

Our Republic would surely founder but for the faith and confidence that we collectively place in our Constitution. And it could not prosper without our diligent commitment to upholding the Constitution's original words and implementing its founding principles. From the noble efforts of public servants to the civic acts of local people, our continuous Constitutional engagement has proved to be an exceptional feature of our Nation's prosperous development.

George W. Bush, "Citizenship Day and Constitution Week Proclamation," September 2001. www.white house.gov/news/releases/2001/09/20010917-15.html.

the Alien and Sedition Act, Madison and Jefferson wrote the Kentucky and Virginia Resolutions. These campaign documents asserted that state governments had the authority to interpose, or declare federal laws unconstitutional. Though the resolutions were never codified into law, they did popularize a new idea about the limits of constitutional authority. Eventually southern states expanded on interposition as a justification for declaring they had the right to dissolve their bonds to the Constitution and secede from the Union. This matter was ultimately resolved by the bloodshed of the Civil War. As a result the North's victory assured that the federal government and the U.S. Constitution would reign supreme. A U.S. Supreme Court decision in *Texas v. White* in 1869 backed up this military solution, asserting, "The Constitution, in all its provisions, looks to an indestructible Union, composed of indestructible States."[66]

Thus, for multiple reasons, the U.S. Constitution is no longer the same document as the one created in Philadelphia in 1789. Perhaps, though, this would not surprise the framers. As nineteenth-century statesman and orator Henry Clay once observed,

"The Constitution of the United States was made not merely for the generation that then existed, but for posterity—unlimited, undefined, endless, perpetual posterity."[67]

Perhaps the greatest attribute of the U.S. Constitution is that it fostered a national identity for a vast nation of immigrants, representing a multitude of races, religions, and creeds from around the world. What continues to bind Americans is a commonly accepted way of life based on a set of principles forged over two hundred years ago by fifty-five extraordinary men. Their genius was that they trusted people to govern themselves.

Notes

Chapter One: The Emergence of the Thirteen Colonies

1. Quoted in William Miller, *A New History of the United States.* New York: George Braziller, 1958, p. 35.
2. Quoted in Miller, *A New History of the United States*, p. 46.
3. Quoted in William Bennett, *America: The Last Best Hope,* vol. 1, *From the Age of Discovery to a World at War, 1492–1914.* Nashville: Nelson Current, 2006, p. 40.
4. Richard B. Morris and Editors of *Life, The New World: Prehistory to 1774.* New York: Time, 1963, p. 119.
5. Paul Johnson, *A History of the American People.* New York: HarperCollins, 1997, p.116.
6. Daniel J. Boorstin, *The Americans: The Colonial Experience.* New York: Random House, 1958, p. 151.
7. David McCullough, *1776.* New York: Simon & Schuster, 2005, p. 23.
8. Quoted in Johnson, *A History of the American People*, p. 137.
9. Quoted in Johnson, *A History of the American People*, p. 137.

Chapter Two: A Growing Rift

10. Quoted in Walter Isaacson, *Benjamin Franklin: An American Life.* New York: Simon & Schuster, 2003, pp. 161–62.
11. Francis D. Cogliano, "Was the American Revolution Inevitable?" British Broadcasting Corporation. bbc.co.uk/history/state/empire/american__revolution__01.shtml.
12. Thomas Fleming, "Little Known Facts About the American Revolutionary War," Official Web Site of the State of Delaware. www.state.de.us/facts/ushisto/revfacts.htm.
13. Howard Zinn, *A People's History of the United States.* New York: Harper & Row, 1980, p. 65.
14. Quoted in Zinn, *A People's History of the United States*, p. 65.
15. Samuel Eliot Morison, *The Oxford History of the American People: Prehistory to 1789.* New York: Penguin, 1991, p. 245.
16. Morison, *The Oxford History of the American People: Prehistory to 1789*, p. 246.

Chapter Three: Revolution!

17. Quoted in McCullough, *1776*, p. 49.
18. Quoted in Isaacson, *Benjamin Franklin: An American Life*, p. 296.
19. Quoted in Sculley Bradley, ed., *The American Tradition in Literature.* New York: Norton & Company, 1967, p. 290.
20. Quoted in George Seldes, *The Great Thoughts.* New York: Ballantine, 1985, p. 319.
21. Quoted in Bennett, *From the Age of Discovery to a World at War, 1492–1914*, p. 82.
22. Quoted in Stephen Ambrose and

Douglas Brinkley, *Witness to America: An Illustrated Documentary History of the United States from the Revolution to Today*. New York: HarperCollins, 1999, p. 17.

23. Quoted in Bennett, *From the Age of Discovery to a World at War, 1492–1914*, p. 86.
24. Quoted in Bennett, *From the Age of Discovery to a World at War, 1492–1914*, p. 86.
25. Quoted in William Miller, *A New History of The United States*. New York: George Braziller, Inc., 1958, p. 94.

Chapter Four: A Young Republic Struggles to Stay Together

26. Quoted in Zinn, *A People's History of the United States*, p. 88.
27. Quoted in Richard B. Morris and Editors of *Life, The Making of a Nation: 1775–1789*. New York: Time, 1963, p. 104.
28. Quoted in Morris and Editors of *Life, The Making of a Nation: 1775–1789*, p. 112.
29. Quoted in Richard Haesly, ed., *The Constitutional Convention*. San Diego: Greenhaven, 2002, p. 45.
30. Quoted in Isaacson, *Benjamin Franklin: An American Life*, p. 445.

Chapter Five: Hammering Out a Constitution

31. Charles Mee, *The Genius of the People*. New York: Harper & Row, 1987, pp. 60–61.
32. Quoted in William Peters, *A More Perfect Union: The Making of the U.S. Constitution*, New York: Crown, 1987, p. 23.
33. Quoted in Morris and Editors of *Life, The Making of a Nation*, p. 131.

34. Quoted in Catherine Drinker Bowen, *Miracle at Philadelphia: The Story of the Constitutional Convention, May to September 1787*. Boston: Little, Brown, 1966, p. 95.
35. Quoted in Mee, *The Genius of the People*, p. 188.
36. Quoted in Isaacson, *Benjamin Franklin: An American Life*, p. 451.
37. Quoted in Bowen, *Miracle at Philadelphia*, p. 131.
38. Quoted in Morris and Editors of *Life, The New World: Prehistory to 1774*, p. 131.
39. Quoted in Mee, *The Genius of the People*, p. 248.
40. Quoted in Mee, *The Genius of the People*, p. 221.
41. Quoted in Peters, *A More Perfect Union: The Making of the U.S. Constitution*, p. 211.
42. Quoted in Peters, *A More Perfect Union: The Making of the U.S. Constitution*, p. 213.
43. Quoted in Peters, *A More Perfect Union: The Making of the U.S. Constitution*, p. 214.

Chapter Six: Ratifying the Constitution

44. Quoted in Roger A. Bruns, *A More Perfect Union: The Creation of the U.S. Constitution: An Introduction*. Washington, DC: National Archives Trust Fund Board, 1986, p. 8.
45. Bowen, *Miracle at Philadelphia*, pp. 271–327.
46. Quoted in Bruns, *A More Perfect Union: The Creation of the U.S. Constitution: An Introduction*, p. 10.
47. Quoted in Bowen, *Miracle at Philadelphia*, pp. 285–86.
48. Morris and Editors of *Life, The New*

World: Prehistory to 1774, p. 134.

49. Peters, *A More Perfect Union: The Making of the U.S. Constitution*, p. 226.

50. Quoted in Bowen, *Miracle at Philadelphia*, p. 293.

51. Quoted in Bowen, *Miracle at Philadelphia*, p. 298.

52. Quoted in Bowen, *Miracle at Philadelphia*, pp. 297–98.

53. Quoted in Peters, *A More Perfect Union: The Making of the U.S. Constitution*, p. 231.

54. Quoted in Bowen, *Miracle at Philadelphia*, pp. 304–305.

55. Peters, *A More Perfect Union: The Making of the U.S. Constitution*, p. 234.

Chapter Seven: An Enduring Document

56. Quoted in B. Davis Schwartz, *The United States Constitution Quotations and Personalities*, Memorial Library, Long Island University. www.liu.edu/CWIS/CWP/LIBRARY/exhibits/constitution/quotes.htm.

57. Quoted in *The United States Constitution Quotations and Personalities*.

58. Stephen Breyer, *Active Liberty: Interpreting Our Democratic Constitution*. New York: Alfred A. Knopf, 2005, p. 32.

59. Breyer, *Active Liberty*, p. 33.

60. Quoted in Alistair Cooke, *America*. New York: Alfred A. Knopf, 1977, p. 146.

61. Quoted in John M. Blum, William S. McFeely, Edmund S. Morgan, Arthur M. Schlesinger Jr., Kenneth M. Stampp, and C. Vann Woodward, *The National Experience: A History of the United States*, 6th ed. San Diego: Harcourt Brace Jovanovich, 1985, p. 336.

62. Breyer, *Active Liberty*, p. 45.

63. Richard B. Morris, "A Few Parchment Pages Two Hundred Years Later, the Constitution 1787–1987." Americanheritage.com. www.americanheritage.com/articles/magzine/ah/19787/4/1987_4_46.shtml.

64. Richard B. Morris, "A Few Parchment Pages."

65. Quoted in Peters, *A More Perfect Union: The Making of the U.S. Constitution*, p. 135.

66. Quoted in Morris, "A Few Parchment Pages."

67. Quoted in *The United States Constitution Quotations and Personalities*.

For Further Reading

Books

Stephen Ambrose and Douglas Brinkley. *Witness to America: An Illustrated Documentary History of the United States from the Revolution to Today.* New York: HarperCollins, 1999. A collection of primary sources arranged in chronological order.

Charles A. Beard and Mary R. Beard, *A Basic History of the United States.* Philadelphia: The Blakiston Company, 1944. A dated, but popular history written by two well-known and controversial historians.

William Bennett, *America: The Last Best Hope, Volume 1: From the Age of Discovery to a World at War, 1492–1914.* Nashville: Nelson Current, 2006. A readable, popular history, by an outspoken political conservative and former U.S. secretary of education.

Sol Bloom, *The Story of the Constitution*, Washington, DC: National Archive and Records Administration, 1986. A reprint of a concise history written by a U.S. congressman for the 150th anniversary of the U.S. Constitution.

John M. Blum, William S. McFeely, Edmund S. Morgan, Arthur M. Schlesinger, Jr., Kenneth M. Stampp, C. Vann Woodward. *The National Experience: A History of the United States, Sixth Edition.* San Diego: Harcourt Brace Jovanovich, 1985. A college-level text book, written by renowned historians.

Daniel J. Boorstin, *The Americans: The Colonial Experience.* New York: Random House, 1958. A scholarly, but interestingly written, reinterpretation of America during its formative years by one of America's renowned historians.

Catherine Drinker Bowen, *Miracle at Philadelphia: The Story of the Constitutional Convention, May to September 1787.* Boston: Little, Brown, 1966. A scholarly yet fascinating and highly readable account of the constitutional convention.

Sculley Bradley, ed. *The American Tradition in Literature.* New York: Norton, 1967. A compendium of American literature from the sixteenth to the nineteenth centuries.

Stephen Breyer, *Active Liberty: Interpreting Our Democratic Constitution.* New York: Alfred A. Knopf, 2005. A Supreme Court justice's explanation of how he uses American principles as a guide to interpreting the Constitution.

Steven C. Bullock, *The American Revolution: A History in Documents.* Oxford, England: Oxford University Press, 2003. A rich collection of primary sources of America's revolutionary era.

Alistair Cooke, *America.* New York: Alfred A. Knopf, 1977. A popular history of America by a well-known English-born broadcast journalist.

Rebecca Brooks Gruver, *An American History, Third Edition, Volume I to 1877*. Reading, Massachusetts: Addison-Wesley, 1981. A college-level history book.

Richard Haesly, ed., *The Constitutional Convention*. San Diego: Greenhaven, 2002. A compilation of primary sources relating to the Constitutional Convention.

Walter Isaacson, *Benjamin Franklin, An American Life*. New York: Simon & Schuster, 2003. A well-written and lively biography of Franklin for a general audience.

Paul Johnson, *A History of the American People*. New York: HarperCollins, 1997. A popular history by a noted politically conservative British writer.

David McCullough, *1776*. Simon & Schuster, 2005. A well-written and fascinating account of the first year of the American Revolution by one of America's favorite historians.

Charles Mee, *The Genius of the People*. New York: Harper & Row, 1987. An insightful history of the Constitutional Convention.

William Miller, *A New History of The United States*. New York: George Braziller, 1958. A readable, witty, scholarly history.

Samuel Eliot Morison, *The Oxford History of the American People, Volume One: Prehistory to 1789*. New York: Penguin Books, 1991. A lively popular history by a Pulitzer Prize–winning historian.

Richard B. Morris and the Editors of *Life*. *The New World: Volume I, Prehistory to 1774*. New York: Time Inc., 1963. A popular and well-written history by a respected historian for a general audience.

————, *The Making of a Nation, Volume II: 1775–1789*. New York: Time Inc., 1963.

William Peters, *A More Perfect Union: The Making of the U.S. Constitution*. New York: Crown, 1987. An interesting and comprehensive history.

Readings in World History, Orlando: Harcourt Brace Jovanovich, 1990. A compilation of primary sources.

George Seldes, *The Great Thoughts*. New York: Ballantine, 1985. A compilation of primary source excerpts from the works of famous people.

Howard Zinn, *A People's History of the United States*. New York: Harper & Row, 1980. A slanted but useful popular history for the general reader that relies heavily on primary sources and quotations to document patterns of exploitation.

Internet Sources

The Annapolis Convention, 1786, from Revolution to Reconstruction. A site filled with primary sources related to American history, created by students of American studies under the guidance of the arts faculty of the University of Groningen in the Netherlands. http://odur.let.rug.nl/~usa/D/1776-1800/constitution/annap.htm.

Roger A. Bruns, "A More Perfect Union: The Creation of the U.S. Constitution, An Introduction: Published for the National Archives and Records Administration by the National Archives Trust Fund Board," 1986. National Archives and Records Administration. www.law.umkc.edu/faculty/projects/ftrials/conlaw/conhist.html.

"Citizenship Day and Constitution Week Proclamation," Citizenship Day and Constitution Week, 2001. By the President of the United States of America,

Proclamation. www.whitehouse.gov/news/releases/ 2001/09/20010917-15.html. The official White House Web site.

Francis D. Cogliano, "Was the American Revolution Inevitable?" The British Broadcast Company Web page, bbc.co.uk/history/state/empire/american__revolution__01.shtml.

The Debates in the Several State Conventions on the Adoption of the Federal Constitution [Elliot's Debates, Volume 1] *in the Federal Convention, Monday, May 28, 1787.* Library of Congress Primary sources, American Memory: http://memory.loc.gov/cgi-bin/query/r?ammem/hlaw:@field(DOCID+@lit(ed00174)).

Thomas Fleming, "Little Known Facts About the American Revolutionary War." The official Web site for the State of Delaware. www.state.de.us/facts/ushisto/revfacts.htm.

Letters of Delegates to Congress, 1774–1789, vol. 1, August 1774–August 1775. John Adams to Abigail Adams. The Library of Congress, American Memory: Primary Documents in American history. www.memory.loc.gov/Ammem/ Ammemhome.html.

Richard B. Morris, "A Few Parchment Pages Two Hundred Years Later. The Constitution, 1787–1987." Americanheritage.com. www.americanheritage.com/articles/magzine/ah/19787/4/1987_4_46.shtml.

The National Archive Experience, The Charter of Freedom, "A New World Is at Hand." United States National Archives online, www.archives.gov/national-archives-experience/charters/constitution_history.html.

"Remarks of Thurgood Marshall"at the 200th Anniversary of the United States Constitution, Maui, Hawaii, May 6, 1987. Civilrights.org, the official Web site of the Leadership Conference on Civil Rights Education Fund and the Leadership Council on Civil Rights. www.civilrights.org/library/permanent_collection/resources/thurgood5687.html

The United States Constitution Quotations and Personalities, Web site of B. Davis Schwartz Memorial Library, Long Island University, www.liu.edu/CWIS/CWP/LIBRARY/exhibits/constitution/quotes.htm.

Index

aid to revolutionaries, 47, 48
colonies in North America, 11, 12, 25
Francis I (king of France), 11
Franklin, Benjamin
    on Albany Plan, 25
    on Constitution, 68
    Constitutional Convention and, 59–60, 61, 70
    Declaration of Independence and, 42
    on making laws, 24
    on signing Declaration of Independence, 43
    signing of Constitution, 75
French and Indian War, 25–29

Gage, Thomas, 31, 36
Gaspee (British ship), 33
Gates, Henry Louis, Jr., 86
Gates, Horatio, 46
George III (king of England), 36, 39, 45
Georgia, 16, 48
Gerry, Elbridge, 68, 75
government, in colonies
    Britain reduced powers of, 34
    colonial, 19
    duty to serve needs of individual, 42
    Enlightenment and, 23–24
    Mayflower Compact, 15
    religion and, 22
    as separate independent, 38
    voting for representation, 29
government, in states
    under Articles of Confederation, 51, 52, 54
    under Constitution, 73, 90–91
government, national
    under Articles of Confederation, 54–57, 58, 59, 78
    under Constitution, 70–71
Granville, Earl, 24
Grayson, William, 81
Great Awakening, 22–23
Great Charter, 20

Habeas Corpus Act (1679), 20
Hamilton, Alexander
    on Articles of Confederation, 58, 59
    at Constitutional Convention, 61, 70
    described, 63
    ratification and, 76, 83
Hancock, John, 43, 80
Harvard University, 23
Henry, Patrick, 64, 81–82
Hessian troops, 45, 64
homes
    British troops quartered in, 28, 31, 35
    of colonists, 18
    searching, 20
Howe, William, 39, 46

Hughes, Charles Evens, 88

indentured servants, 16, 51
independence
    call for, by Paine, 40, 41
    call for, denied, 35–36, 39
    declared, 41–43, 51–52
Indians. *See* Native Americans
Intolerable Acts, 35
Iroquois Indians, 25

Jamestown, VA, 12–14
Jay, John, 64, 76
Jefferson, Thomas
    Constitutional Convention and, 64
    Declaration of Independence and, 42
    on government under Articles of Confederation, 56
    Kentucky and Virginia Resolutions, 90–91
Jews, 22
John (king of England), 20
Johnson, Paul, 23
judicial review, 88–90

Kentucky Resolutions, 90–91
King, Rufus, 70
King's College, 23
Knox, Henry, 38

land ownership and voting, 19
Lee, Richard Henry, 41
Lexington, MA, 36
Lincoln, Abraham, 90
Locke, John, 24, 42
Louis XVI (king of France), 47

Madison, James
    on anti-federalists, 77
    Bill of Rights and, 83
    Constitutional Convention and, 59, 61, 64, 65
    Kentucky and Virginia Resolutions, 90–91
    ratification and, 76
Magna Carta, 20
Maryland, 15, 81
Mason, George, 61, 75
Massachusetts
    African Americans in, 53
    farmers' rebellion in, 58
    ratification convention, 80–81
    see also specific cities
Massachusetts Bay Colony, 15
Mayflower Compact, 15
McCullough, David, 23
Mee, Charles, 61
Middle Colonies, 16, 18
    see also Philadelphia, PA

Picture Credits

About the Author

John M. Dunn is a freelance writer and high school history teacher. He has taught in Georgia, Florida, North Carolina, and Germany. As a writer and journalist, he has published numerous articles and stories in more than twenty periodicals, as well as scripts for audiovisual productions and a children's play. His books *The Russian Revolution*, *The Relocation of the North American Indian*, *The Spread of Islam*, *Advertising*, *The Civil Rights Movement*, *The Enlightenment*, *Life During the Black Death*, *The Vietnam War: A History of U.S. Involvement*, *The Computer Revolution*, *The French Revolution: The Fall of the Monarchy*, and *Castro's Cuba*, are published by Lucent Books. He lives with his wife and two daughters in Ocala, Florida.